Clash of Cultures

Clash of Cultures

A Psychodynamic Analysis of Homer and the Iliad

Vincenzo Sanguineti

LEXINGTON BOOKS
Lanham • Boulder • New York • London

Published by Lexington Books
An imprint of The Rowman & Littlefield Publishing Group, Inc.
4501 Forbes Boulevard, Suite 200, Lanham, Maryland 20706
www.rowman.com

6 Tinworth Street, London SE11 5AL, United Kingdom

Copyright © 2021 by The Rowman & Littlefield Publishing Group, Inc.

All rights reserved. No part of this book may be reproduced in any form or by any electronic or mechanical means, including information storage and retrieval systems, without written permission from the publisher, except by a reviewer who may quote passages in a review.

British Library Cataloguing in Publication Information Available

Library of Congress Cataloging-in-Publication Data Available

ISBN 978-1-7936-4405-3 (cloth)
ISBN 978-1-7936-4407-7 (pbk)
ISBN 978-1-7936-4406-0 (electronic)

Timeo Danaos et dona ferentis (Virgil, Aeneidos II, l. 49)

Contents

Foreword		ix
	Donatella Marazziti	
Introduction		1
1	The Author	5
2	The Epic and Its Coming to Life	17
3	Homer and the Greeks	29
4	Book II: A Dynamic Analysis of the Opposing Armies	55
5	Book XIX: The Transferred Wrath against the Trojans	63
6	Concluding the Analysis on the Opening Demands	85
7	Homer and the Trojans	97
8	Homer and the Orient: Integrating Psychodynamics and History	107
Appendix A		111
Appendix B: *Iliad* Books: A Synopsis		117
Bibliography		123
Index		125
About the Author		133

Foreword

Donatella Marazziti

After more than two millennia, the *Iliad* continues to be one of the most intriguing poems eliciting debates, discussions and controversies worldwide. With no doubt, we should reflect on what our Western culture might be without it (and without the subsequent *Odyssey*). My feeling is that I would feel orphaned, orphaned of a part of me, not only of my cultural domain, but mostly of my feelings and passions.

Therefore, the crucial question is: why does *Iliad* involve us so much? Why does it scramble us so in depth? Why do we participate in and share the pains, sorrows or joys of its heroes and of more or less visible protagonists?

Throughout the centuries, writers, poets, teachers, philosophers, and sociologists tried to address these and other important questions even regarding the origin and the "hand" who wrote the poem, while offering different explanations and interpretations, that are somehow partial or subjective.

In his book, *Clash of Cultures*, Dr. Vincenzo Sanguineti, with his peculiar background and sensitivity, coupled with, last but not least, classical culture (too often neglected nowadays), first assumes that Homer was the writer of the *Iliad*. As a result, he tried to explore his conscious, subconscious, rational and emotional drives, as well his context and time.

According to Dr. Sanguineti, Homer is a son of his time whose family had to migrate in order to escape from war and destructions. I fully agree with this opinion, as in the *Iliad* it is evident Homer's longing for a previous way of life: according to me, this is the strongest feeling of the *Iliad*, even stronger than in the *Odyssey*. That's why, while in the *Odyssey*, the hero fights to go back home and, at the end, he is able to accomplish his scope and desire, the *Iliad* is permeated by the sad awareness that a civilization, that of Homer's family and where probably he had grown up, is going to an end and will never resurrect, while being destroyed by a new, more aggressive and powerful culture imposing new values and way of life. It is interesting to underline that the word "nostalgy" derives from the two Greek words "νόστος, nostos = return" and "ἄλγος, algos = pain," so that it literally means "pain of the return." And Homer perfectly knows there is no possibility of any return to his previous life and world.

This may also explain why his warm attitude and emotional participations is directed towards the defeated Trojans.

I must confess that, when I was a student at the high school and studied the *Iliad* in ancient Greek, the most sticky, emotional and vivid image I had (and still have) in my mind, was the last parting of Hector from Andromache and their little Astyanax, as I "felt" Hector's awareness of his next death and the sunset of an entire civilization.

With no doubt, the interpretation that Dr. Sanguineti puts forward for the *Iliad*, is not only original, but also comprehensive and modern, as he is the first to underline the relationships between emotions, feelings and cognitions of the writer, Homer, and his historical, contextual background and Zeitgeist.

If it is true that the *Iliad*'s characters derive from inner archetypes, according to Jung's theory (that Dr. Sanguineti knows well, while being a psychiatrist, a neuroscientist and a psychoanalytically oriented therapist), this probably explains why this poem continues to be so attractive, powerful and so close to us, as they provoke vibrations that are embedded in our human nature and our brains share with all members of our species. However, it is also true that the *Iliad* is a product resulting from the melting of Homer's sensitivity and subjectivity with his time and cultural values.

I must add that the title of Sanguineti's book *Clash of Cultures* is also extremely current, so that it unavoidably stimulates me to reflect on the evidence that nowadays the separation and conflicts between Western and Eastern cultures do persist, and may sometimes lead to aggressive deeds, such as terrorism acts. I wonder why after millennia and ferocious wars, it seems so difficult to reach an integration respectful of cultural differences and trying to alleviate the "nostalgy" of those who are forced to migrate from their countries to other distant ones.

For this reason, I consider it an honor and a privilege to introduce *Clash of Cultures* written by my friend and distinguished colleague Dr. Vincenzo Sanguineti, as the impact of his book will be not limited to the interpretation of the *Iliad*, but will promote reflections on unresolved intercultural clashes still present nowadays.

—Dr. Donatella Marazziti
Prof. of Psychiatry, University of Pisa and Professor of Psychology,
Unicamillus University of Rome, Italy

Map of the Aegean Sea. Created by Kate Otte.

Introduction

Between 900 and 700 BC a blind—or so one story goes[1]—Greek bard named Homer collected and/or composed, possibly in a pre-literate, oral form, an epic called the *Iliad*, which eventually was organized in 24 books by the Alexandria Head Librarian Zenodotus of Ephesus, and which was allegedly declaimed at various Courts in the ancient Greek world. A brief synopsis of the 24 books, their content and main characters, is presented in Appendix B.

A current popular assessment of the *Iliad* would probably describe it as an ancient Greek poem, written by a blind Greek poet, about a war in a faraway city called Troy, to rescue the fabulous Helen, "the face (read breasts[2]) who launched a thousand ships"; the great, invulnerable Achilles was its greatest hero; after a quarrel with the Chief Commander Agamemnon, he eventually killed the Trojan prince Hector, and dragged his body attached to his chariot, enraged by the fact that Hector had killed his friend-cousin-lover Patroclus (the assessment may also mention the wooden horse!).

In fact, for over two millennia the *Iliad* has been seen as a powerful description of the tragedies of war, and as a major acclaim to the military supremacy of Greece upon Asia, expressed through the aristeias of several great Greek heroes, as those of Diomedes, Agamemnon, Patroclus, and the prototypical one of Achilles starting in Book XX. The epic was a foreword to the feats against the Persians that, a few centuries later, stunned even the very Greeks, fatally injured Persia's might and pride, and served as a prelude for the rise and the extraordinary Eastern campaign of Alexander the Great.

Sometime after the *Iliad*—or so the story carries on—Homer put together a second epic, the *Odyssey*: the saga of Odysseus' return home and his aristeia (he had not received one in the *Iliad*), interspersed with various adventures by sea, recollections of the war, and the fate of its major players.

The details of the ancient oral performance of both epics, and their conversions to the written form, inspire continual debate among scholars.

Whoever composed the *Odyssey* was moved by the figure of Odysseus, whom the author used as the central character to a series of tales. Apart from the first four books (the Telemachy) describing Telemachus' journey to find his father, one encounters the Apologoi, or the tale that Odysseus told the Phaeacians about his peregrinations since he left the island of Calypso. It incorporates the Cyclopeia—the adventure against Polyphemus and the wrath of Poseidon—and the Nekuia, or his journey to Hades to find the blind seer Tiresias. The epic culminates with the Mnesterophonia, Odysseus' powerful aristeia and slaying of the suitors of his wife, Penelope. Possibly, these tales were integrated during the Classical period around 300 BC into the single epic, and, by the same Zenodotus, significantly organized also in 24 books, as the *Iliad* was.

The reading of the two works has always generated in me different types of feelings, with the *Odyssey* being much more entertaining and full of captivating adventures, some highly fantastic and filled with magical events and characters,[3] but lacking the depth of tragedy that permeates the *Iliad* where so much is at stake, from the fate of myriads of men to that of entire civilizations. The reader of the *Odyssey* reviews those tragedies, through Odysseus' narrative, against the vivid background of the compelling journey, but from a distance, so to speak. Overall, the *Iliad* appears to be a more complicated epic poem than the *Odyssey*, and this impression has supported the opinion of several scholars that the two works are the products of different authors, although both closely related to the Epic Cycle.

I join the majority of the Homeric scholars in disagreeing; Homer's innate skills as storyteller and in capturing individual personalities diffuse both works. They differ in that the *Iliad* is a tragedy carrying the gravitas of collective themes that involve both human and suprahuman systems, while the *Odyssey* is an adventure-laden allegory of a personal journey to self-actualization, which probably capitalized on the success of the first epic. The difference between the two works may also be reflected in the fact that among the vast body of manuscripts about Homer that have accumulated during the past two millennia, the *Iliad* is constantly favored over the *Odyssey* by 2:1 or better.[4]

The group of works known as the Epic Cycle consisted of several epic poems dealing with material from the Mycenaean Bronze Age culture and related to the story of the Trojan War. Of the several works— the Cypria, the Aethiopis, the Little Iliad, the Iliupersis, the Nostoi, and the Telegony— only fragments and brief summaries have survived. In his Chrestomathia the author, Proclus, mentions that at least another work preceded the Cypria, suggesting a very rich landscape of sagas and compositions coloring that historical era, among which Homer stands as the sole survivor.

The title of my book indicates that it will have a different approach to the *Iliad* than most previous scholarly ones. It will describe the psychodynamic framework of Homer and of his creation. The rationale for this study will gradually emerge with the progression of the analysis. As an introduction, it will suffice to present in general terms the procedure and its main objectives and characteristics. In the words of Dr. Cabaniss, from the Department of Psychiatry at Columbia University, "a psychodynamic formulation is a hypothesis about the way a person's unconscious thoughts and feelings"[5] may be participating in the person's conscious mental activities. Furthermore, always in the words of Dr. Cabaniss, "using a psychodynamic technique is ... also about understanding how and why those unconscious thoughts and feelings developed" along the evolving journey of that mind, from early, infantile, primarily affect-laden experiences to their more mature elaborations of adulthood.

The importance of a psychodynamic, rather than a static, understanding of those fifty-one Iliadic summer days, and of the author of the saga will become clear as my research will explore at progressively greater psychological depths the complex unconscious and subconscious, cognitive and affective vicissitudes of Homer and of the Trojan tragedy; and the approach will add a valuable complementary dimension to Homer and the *Iliad*.

A multidimensional methodology, that would include also the dimension of time, is an important requirement in order to achieve a more comprehensive grasp of the most important extant work of literary art that came to us from such an ancient past.

Usually the *Iliad* is approached as a story of <u>what</u> happened, and Homer, the bard who composed that particular story, has been conceptualized by subsequent scholars on the basis and as a reflection of the story's overt content. A psychodynamic formulation, however, offers a hypothesis of <u>why</u> things happened and why a mind came to imagine them the way it did; the focus shifts from the *Iliad* and its content to Homer and his mental landscape. In the words of Dr. Cabaniss, "a psychodynamic formulation is more than a story; it is a narrative that tries to explain how and why people think."[6] It is an attempt to get an idea of what shaped the way to a specific outcome.

Mine is a psychodynamic analysis of the final collection of words that are attributed to Homer, as they were preserved by the Alexandrine librarians—among many others—over two millennia ago, along their journey from oral conception to textual codification.

Its scope is to revisit the main narratives that form the scaffoldings of the *Iliad* and to search for cognitive and affective elements in the same narratives that would offer plausible pointers to their overt and covert dynamic processes, and explain "how and why people think": what inspired and offered meanings to the crucial events and characters of the epic.

The search for meaningful material that may shed light on hidden, suppressed or truly unconscious information does necessarily require a very detailed, often repetitious, analysis of potential indicators carrying some sort of cathecting coloring that alerts the analyst's attention. This will represent most of the present work: initially collecting the different sets of available data, then looking for a narrative that would connect them, and eventually formulating a psychodynamic interpretation out of each narrative.

Due to the fact that Homer and the *Iliad* operate at two different but heavily intertwined levels, the human and the divine, the analysis of their psychic organization relies loosely on the structural and topographical Freudian models as well as on the archetypal model of Jung.

Clearly, this is not a scholastic study of Homer and his works, their origins, stylistic values, ownerships, chronologies, and so on. I would not be qualified for such a task, nor able to add anything of significance to the vast body of diverse studies that have been conducted on this figure and his putative works.

The same caveat applies to the material I used. Each narrative required information on its longitudinal development through time, in order to allow for a better understanding of its dynamics. My choice of original sources reflects the limits of my search, as well as my concern to avoid as much as possible any "countertransferential" revisionism from subsequent sociocultural basins, possibly affectively too remote from the original events, and even dystonic to their significance. While ancient reports carry already their own revisionism—as later memories of past events in the therapeutic encounter often do—their relative proximity and affective linkage to the source may provide better reliability about the dynamics of specific events than the one offered by the reconstructions from minds affectively distant, disconnected from the Homeric Zeitgeist.

NOTES

1. ...whenever any one of men on the earth, a stranger who has seen and suffered much, comes here and asks of you: "whom think ye, girls, is the sweetest singer that comes here, and in whom do you most delight?" Then answer, each and all, with one voice: "He is a blind man, and dwells in rocky Chios: his lays are evermore supreme." Homeric Hymn to Delian Apollo, vv 165 ff. (Hesiod, The Homeric Hymns and Homerica).
2. Little Iliad, 13 (Hesiod, LCL, # 57 p. 519).
3. The magical dimension is practically absent from the *Iliad*, either as actual occurrences or as recollections of magical events. There are some divine interventions that fall within the traditional parameters of what the Gods can do; but nowhere could one find a character in the sustained role of a sorceress and enchantress as Circe, who is a central figure from book X to book XII of the *Odyssey*! Or the magical ships of the Phaeacians (*Odyssey*, Book VIII, ll. 555 ff.), which are a cross between ancient sorcery and super modern high-level, science fictional A.I., in that "the ships themselves understand the thoughts and minds of men, and know the cities..." The sentient computer HAL in the in movie "2001: A Space Odyssey" was their modern equivalent!
4. *A New Companion to Homer*, pp. 60-61.
5. *Psychodynamic Formulation*, p. 4.
6. Ibid., p. 6.

ONE
The Author

Which brings us to the figure of Homer, the Bard of the West, who provided the foundations of the Western Canon.[1]

A figure of myth, his very birth is shrouded in mystery; and yet, the location in time of his figure and of his creation, even if approximate, and its relationship to the date of the fall of Troy, so gravid in meaning and by predominant consensus set around the middle of the twelfth century BC,[2] may be of great significance in activating within our psyche some resonance for Homer's "spirit of his time," and to capture a glimpse of the dynamic unfolding of his psyche.

Jung, in the first section of his Red Book, the Liber Primus, under the heading "The way of what is to come," refers with the term "spirit of the time" to the sociocultural basin in which we are all immersed, quite intricately and mostly unconsciously. Each era has a specific "spirit," a Zeitgeist, that forms its collective rational mind, its value system and its moral code. He then continues his self-exploration and his self-disclosure by adding: "I have learned that in addition to the spirit of this time there is still another spirit at work, namely that which rules the depths of everything contemporary." He labels this different set of knowledge "the spirit of the depth" and goes on describing how "from time immemorial and for all the future (it) possesses a greater power than the spirit of this time, who changes with the generations. He forced me down to the last and simplest things . . . took my understanding and all my knowledge and placed them at the service of the inexplicable and the paradoxical." [C. Jung. Liber Novus (fol.1, r.)]

Jung refers here to the domain of the archetypes, those cognitive and affective configurations that represent the world of the organizing templates and are untouched by the passage of time.

These concepts of Jung correspond, in a different metaphorical form, to the "unconscious consciousness" of neuroscientist Antonio Damasio who compares the knowledge of the Ego to the knowledge of the brain (or self, in psychological terms); he enumerates its unconscious content[3] and concludes the list with the comment: "Amazing indeed, how little we consciously ever know." Both the formulations of Jung and of Damasio expand the mental landscape beyond the insights of Freud, who had limited the archetypal domain to the libidinal and sexual drives.

Our ability to open those windows in the past would allow us to extricate ourselves somewhat from our own socio-cultural basin, and to connect through the millennia, stirred by the deep collective sense of our basic humanity across cultures and generations: the domain of the Jungian spirit of the depth and its archetypal dynamics. The derivatives of those eternal organizing factors form the matrix supporting all manifestations of mental life and our potential for true active imagination (these being some of the elements out of which the perennial power of myth finds its energy).

Therefore, a major concern of the entire procedure has been the need to abandon the present sociocultural milieu and enter the one of Homer and his era. While three thousand years appear like too vast a gulf between ours and Homer's mind, on second thought the process is less affected by chronological factors than by the diversity of individualized, subjective expressions of diverse socio-cultural value systems, irrespective of their location along the chronological continuum. Across the differences in discourse of the various spirits of the time one encounters the commonalities inherent to the spirit of the depth, the archetypal messages that transcend the phenotypical social diversity and allow for empathic connectivity to common and universal concepts. This approach is consistent with intersubjective psychotherapy, in which the analyst experiences the analysand's subjective domain while sheltering the process from any influence or interpretation based on one's own subjectivity and countertransferential bias.

The first two centuries following the fall of Troy were highly destabilized, possibly in ways that had never been experienced before. Empires and kingdoms fell, from the Euphrates to the Gulf of Corinth. A strong wave of expansionism from Greece dotted with colonies the eastern shores of the Mediterranean Sea. Profound cultural and religious shifts were imposed, often reinforced by the threat of the sword. It is hard for us to imagine the effect of those changes on the psyche of a rural, agrarian population, scattered in largely isolated congregations directing their lives primarily on oral traditions and local beliefs. Prof. K. Raaflaub, in his essay on Homeric society,[4] comments that by the end of the second millennium BC. "The general impression remains one of a massively reduced population living in small and scattered villages, in simple conditions and relative isolation." A grasp at this dimension, though, is crucial to any attempt to visualize the collective "spirit" of those times, in that communal memories of the past, in particular of great traumas and great achievements, and their effect on coloring the emotional substrate in the collective psyche of affected systems, span through generations.[5] The Confederate spirit one century and a half after the end of the Secession War still colors the affective disposition of large segments of the South toward the blue coats Yankee colonizers, and feeds their lament for the disappearance of a specific sociocultural pattern of being and living. Over five centuries separate modern Peru from the final collapse of the Inca Empire, but to the Inca descendants the memory of the dark, exceedingly brutal Spanish colonization, which tried to obliterate the very culture and existence of the people while raping its women and pillaging its assets, is still deeply felt and a source of ongoing smoldering hostility and resentment.

This transgenerational power of collective memories needs to be kept in mind, when evaluating Homer and the meaning of his works, both being colored by the effect of the Trojan defeat upon his motherland. I use here the term "motherland" because tradition describes Homer as born at Smyrna or on the small island of Chios, off the coast of Anatolia (see map). There is no mention anywhere, in the scholastic studies about his figure, that he was born in mainland Greece or that his developing mind was affected in any significant degree by being a Greek-born citizen nourished by a collective value system of mainland Greece.[6] Rather, the scanty available data about him tend to define the sociocultural basin of his early development as that specific area of western Anatolia bordering the kingdom of Troy. Information about his parents comes from those writings collectively known as The Lives of Homer.[7] All of them identify the mother as a young woman named Cretheis. Pseudo-Herodotus—who composed a highly embellished and imaginific story of Homer's life—reports that she had become pregnant after a "secret intercourse" and was sent out of shame to Smyrna, where she eventually worked as a laborer for a man who allegedly promised to take care of her child in exchange for her coming to live with him. Pseudo-Plutarch mentions that she was either of Smyrna or forced to settle down there because of an illegitimate pregnancy, and he names her brother Maion as the father by rape, while for Proclus Maion was a husband and legitimate father (he does not name the mother). All these sources report that Cretheis called her son Melesigenes because she delivered him near the banks of the local river Meles (a tale by Castricius of Nicaea, as reported by Hesychius of Miletus, transforms the mother into a local nymph, and the father into the god river himself[8]). At some time, while still a very small child, he may have been given as a hostage (ὅμηρος or omeros) when the Smyrnaeans were threatened with a war against the Colophonians or the Chians; and that became his name.[9]

All this material has some importance when trying to formulate his psychodynamic profile. The information suggests that Homer had a complex and stressful infancy and childhood, possibly without a father and with a mother struggling as a laborer or subject to an obligated relationship, out of dire necessity more than free choice. These infantile experiences may very well be the psychodynamic antecedents to scenes and comments that will emerge in the *Iliad*, as I will illustrate during the analysis.

The importance of the impact that early traumatic experiences exert on the psychic development of a child and how they mold his or her mental landscape cannot be emphasized enough. These memory traces are primarily of a feeling nature and are heavily loaded with enduring, analogical affective content that may not transpire in the logical narrative and yet pervades and colors its unconscious depth. Even after a superficial healing these affective memories can erupt to the surface at any time, given sufficient activation, as we will see in the case of Patroclus and his tragic pull to the dark side.

At the time of the Trojan War, the two putative birth sites of Smyrna or Chios were part of the kingdom of the Seha River Lands, allied to the great nation of Hatti and probably ruled by King Mashturi, a brother-in-law of the Hittite Emperor Muwatalli.

It had been a kingdom with a rich and proud history, even in its dealings with the vastly superior empire of Hatti, sharing this history with the contiguous kingdom of Troy to the North, and the distant kingdom of Lycia (or Lukka) at the Southern end of the Anatolian Western seaboard. It had—or so the legend goes—taken the brunt of the first misdirected Greek expedition led by Agamemnon[10] that—so legend also goes—was saved from an ignominious defeat by the exploits of fifteen-year-old Achilles, who wounded the Mysian king Telephus.[11]

Even the campaigns of conquest by Hatti had respected the fabric and the customs of the entire seaboard region, although some of the kingdoms had become just a pretense of the original ones, garrisoned by Hittite strongholds and with kings chosen for their acquiescence to the Hittite emperor. Despite all its oppression, Hatti could also be a safeguard against Greek economic and armed expansionism, as when the Hittite emperor Tudhaliya sent troops to protect Madduwatta, a local vassal ruler, from the Achaean invader Attarssiya.[12] Already around 1300 BC the complaints of a Hittite emperor to a Greek (Achaean) counterpart testify to the aggressive behavior of Greece toward the population of western Anatolia.[13]

With the fall of Troy and its allies, and, shortly afterwards, the disintegration of the Hittite empire, all bastions to the Greek easterly expansionistic push disappeared and a major wave of Greek colonization gradually swept along the entire Anatolian coast, due also to pressure from political instability in mainland Greece.

As mentioned already, nothing could be found in the scanty records about Homer to suggest that his parents were part of these early waves of immigrants. It is as likely that Homer was the offspring of local laborers, if not actually the fatherless child of a laborer-captive woman, and grew up as a subject citizen under Greece, well versed in the language[14] and culture of the colonial power. He may have been the repository of shared feelings and images from the legendary history of his homeland, the once great nation along the Seha River, with its proud kings; those feelings and those images were different from the ones preferred by the colonial power, centered on the primacy of the Grecian motherland.

Several factors, in part fully beyond our present limited understanding, affected the strength of the libidinal cathexis of those images and feelings, including the inverse relationship between their cathected energy and the extent of time separating the war from Homer's period. It follows that some perception of the chronological relationship between the war of Troy and the life of Homer would allow us to better assess the type and the vitality of the dynamic forces operating on Homer's mental development and cascading into his creation, and on the collective spirit of his time.

The chronology of Homer's life is usually deducted from the dating of the *Iliad*, which is deducted from the study of the type of written Greek that appears in the extant manuscripts; and here things may get somewhat complicated.

A line of studies to assess with some precision the time when the *Iliad* was written, as suggested by its prevalent use of letters and words, is based on the relationship of its written forms to the samples of a very archaic Greek, called Linear B, that had been used in clay tablets recording primarily lists of possessions, and that is the earliest attested form of written Greek, predating the Greek alphabet by several centuries. It consists of around 87 syllabic signs and over 100 ideographic signs. These ideograms or "signifying" signs symbolize objects or commodities.[15] Prof. R. Janko[16] ran a careful study of the relationship between these syllabic elements, the text of the *Iliad*, and its dating. Interestingly, when discussing his lifework in his biography he comments that: "my results are sometimes travestied by those who hold that I argue that the *Iliad* was taken down in precisely 750 BC and the *Odyssey* in 733 BC. All I in fact did was to show what happens if we adopt different hypotheses about absolute dates and rates of linguistic change, because the relative sequence of the poems is fixed. Thus, Homer must be older than Hesiod."[17]

A compounding issue appears to be the fact that, as far as I know, the oldest extant versions of the *Iliad* are the ones contained in the famous Venetus A and Venetus B manuscripts.[18] The two manuscripts eventually arrived to Italy in the middle 1400s AD and were donated by the Greek scholar Cardinal Bessarion to the Republic of Venice (from which they get their name), part of the Bibliotheca Marciana, where they stayed largely forgotten until the late 1700s.

The earlier peregrinations of these texts are worth some consideration. The copying of Venetus A is attributed to Aristarchus of Samothrace (220–143 BC), Grammarian and Head Librarian (153 BC) at the Library of Alexandria. He is described as a pedantic and fastidious scholar, with a vigilant eye for metrical correctness, prone to reject doubtful lines, and careful to follow, for the critical analysis of the text, the accent system proposed by his teacher Aristophanes of Byzantium (257–185 BC), who had been the preceding Head Librarian (207 BC) after he had succeeded the Head Librarian Eratosthenes of Cyrene (276–195 BC), and who had likely copy-edited the manuscript himself.

These last two head librarians had been mentored or inspired by Zenodotus of Ephesus (ca. 325–260 BC), who had been the first Superintendent of the Library and the first critical editor of Homer, although his knowledge of the Greek language was considered insufficient to the task. His editing was arbitrary; he expunged verses, transposed lines, introduced new readings. As already mentioned, he was probably the one who organized in twenty-four books the *Iliad* as well as the *Odyssey*. No regular Homeric commentaries of his have survived, but he may have been the source of the Homeric "glossai," the glosses or list of unusual words.[19]

It is plausible that these scholars, guided by the spirit of their age, were faced with old texts that showed the eroding signs of time passing, handwritten on papyri or other perishable material, with archaic words or spellings or images that appeared to be products of poor scribing, some even seen as unsuitable to the current audiences or blemishes to the purity of the epic, to be corrected if not fully expunged. While rewriting and refurbishing the old texts, the scholars performed their version of revisionism (a trend, with all its mostly obscure psychodynamics, that has continued to express its pull and its seductiveness throughout the ages).[20]

The ultimate significance of the linguistic variables in the chronological coding of the *Iliad* may therefore change considerably when all the other potential variables emerging from the dynamics of those particular sociocultural basins are added to the equation and magnify the complexity of the context under observation.

The difficulty of searching for a chronological location of Homer grows exponentially if one takes into consideration Homer as an original pre or proto-literal rhapsode,[21] who gathered the material that he needed for his orally declaimed *Iliad* out of the broad flow of images and recollections generated by the Trojan affair and its related stories and reports (out of this same flow other rhapsodes collected what suited their particular interests, ultimately organizing their material in the various epics of the cycle[22]). In a societal system communicating primarily, if not exclusively,[23] by word of mouth, the conflagration around Troy and the final defeat of the Trojans and their allies in a destructive sea of blood and flames were of a magnitude never seen before.[24] From early on the amount of available oral reporting and storytelling must have been quite significant; with the passing of time, repetitions, corrections, and idiosyncratic embellishments contributed to the variable level of reliability or fantasy to be found in the material.

The hypothesis of an unwritten art of poetry at the origin of the Homeric epics was first advanced by Prof. Milman Parry in the 1920s and evolved in the so-called Oral Formulaic Theory, which contrasted, in depicting the figure of Homer, with the calculations based on the linguistic studies of the extant *Iliad* and *Odyssey* manuscripts. These studies required the exclusion of older oral forms of the epic that would have been consistent with the tradition of the oral rhapsodes. In his introduction to his translation of the *Iliad*, Murray reports how Parry showed that the method of composition of the epic, with its often-repeated metrical phrases or "formulas," resembled the practice of illiterate bards, the singer-poets or aoidoi of ancient Greece, and therefore could not be judged by the criteria of written literature.

Prof. John Foley, in his essay "Oral tradition and its implications,"[25] (where he explores in some detail the structure of the Oral Theory), describes how Parry advanced the hypothesis of a Homeric oral tradition, with the Homeric poems representing "the culmination of a process that brought the stories from probable roots in the Mycenean period, through the textless Dark Age, to their eventual recording. The most important vehicle was neither tablet not papyrus . . . but the spoken word." If true, this scenario would push the composition of the *Iliad* further in the past than the analysis of the written versions would allow. Therefore, I will report a few considerations from his essay that are significant to an expanded understanding of the developmental dynamics of the *Iliad* and of the positioning of Homer along the arc of time that followed the Trojan War.

Finding supporting confirmation in the current preliterate South Slavic epic tradition, Parry—and then his assistant, Lord—interpreted Homer's dependence on the frequent and repetitive formulaic language "as being useful to the composing poet because the formulas were part of his poetic tradition." In addition, through the analysis of the heroic songs of the South Slavs, "he provided a detailed description of the apprenticeship of the singer, from the time the young boy first becomes interested in performance through his mature appropriation of the craft."[26]

Lord also analyzed the masterpiece of the Slavic singer Avdo Medjedovic, *The Wedding of Smailagic Meho*, consisting of 12,311 lines. "Here was living proof, Lord reasoned, that traditional oral epic could reach Homeric proportions in the hands of a talented singer, proof that the inherited and shared compositional style could yield a poem of imposing size and rewarding depth."[27]

We will probably never know when the Homeric poems started to be orally-dictated and became ultimately textualized, and as a consequence their performance arenas ceased to be physical realities. However, the presence of an ancient oral tradition in the background of the epics and preceding their transformation into textually fixed poems requires a re-setting of the appearance of Homer, placing him at some earlier times than the dates inferred by the written material, and closer to the Trojan events and the political changes in the region. The repositioning of Homer along the arc of time that followed the Trojan War helps also to understand the relative intensity of the emotional impact that the event continued to exercise on the local population and at what stage in its aftereffects did Homer appear on the scene. An expanded understanding of the sociocultural and geopolitical variables surrounding him plays a significant role in an expanded understanding of Homer as a human figure and of the priorities that may have guided his psychological development and his creative attitude.

The direct input from two ancient historians may add further information to the data offered by the "lives of Homer." Herodotus studied the topic of Homer's location in time and assessed—on unreported research—that the poet lived around the middle of the ninth century BC; Pseudo Herodotus calculated that Homer must have lived not later than 150 years after the Trojan War.[28] These data would locate Homer between two and four generations after the fall of the city.[29]

We have once more to ask ourselves: what sort of legends about the deeds at Troy caught the imagination of that young boy growing up in Smyrna or Chios? How did the collective psyche of his putative homeland integrate the memories of its legendary past and of that ancient conflict in the neighboring kingdom? If he was a colonized subject under a system that tended to strongly impose the values of Greece as the rule of the day it may have been difficult, and risky, to openly declaim any longing for the glories and inspirations on one's past legacy.[30] After all, "Hellenization" was demanded of all its "barbarian" subjects, together with loyalty. The harsh aspect of Greek colonization could still be observed as recently as 400 BC, nine centuries after the first recorded complaint about their behavior in the Tawagalawa letter reported above. The enlightened democratic Athenians proved that harshness upon the island of Melos, which had sided with Sparta. They invaded the island, killed all adult males, sold all women and children as slaves, and replaced the entire local population with their own people.[31] The psychodynamics of Homer's mind (the *Iliad* being the expression of such mind) as the product of his times, rather than of our times, play a crucial part in searching the meanings that may have guided the author. When one approaches the *Iliad* from the alternative perspective of a poem that may have been born out of the mind of a colonized subject, under a power with fundamentally different customs and religious attitudes, a power that would not hesitate to use exile, slavery and death as responses to unwelcome behaviors and suspicion of disloyalty, then the epic may at least require an alternate reading, looking for alternate interpretations.

It is therefore justifiable, on the basis of the data collected so far, to envision, side by side with the Greek bard, another Homer invested in describing the saga of a city trapped in the saga of a war—the city representing vestiges of his homeland and of its cultural inheritance, and the war being its destructive counterpart. Perhaps in the *Iliad* there is hidden also some sub-rosa meaning, running side by side with the overt Greek saga, that would escape any reader captured in the present collective interpretation of the epic as a message of Western military everlasting glory and cultural predominance, Achilles being its undiscussed prototype.

This option would be in some alignment with the concepts expressed by Prof. S. Morris in her essay "Homer and the Near East."[32] She explored material indicative of a relationship between the Homeric and Epic Cycle narratives and elements of Bronze Age Near Eastern cultures, with which they share historical and mythological elements.

Centuries of oral performances preceded the written form of the *Iliad*, which was "harvested from a rich heritage of stories long alive in the Bronze Age and in the Near East, reconstituted into an epic tradition of uniquely Greek heroic dimensions."[33] (Prof. Morris's essay on the connection between Homer and the Near East will be revisited at the conclusion of the book.)

NOTES

1. The Western canon is the body of Western literature, European classical music, philosophy, and works of art that represents the high culture of Europe and North America.

2. Eratosthenes in his Chronographiai (now lost) set the date at 1184–1183 BC.

3. "(I) all the fully formed images to which we do not attend; (II) all the neural patterns that never become images; (III) all the dispositions that were acquired through experience, lie dormant, and may never become an explicit neural pattern; (IV) all quiet remodeling of such dispositions and all their quiet renetworking; (V) all the hidden wisdom and know-how that nature embodied in innate homeostatic dispositions'" *The Feeling of What Happens*, p. 228.

4. *A New Companion to Homer*, pp. 624 ff.

5. In the same essay Prof. Raaflaub proposes that "In preliterate societies, collective memories of the past are preserved beyond a period of roughly three generations only if they are important to the present," as certainly the memories of the Trojan war and its aftereffects had to be for the local population.

6. We are left to consider the curious fact that the *Iliad*, the most outstanding opus praising Bronze Age Mycenaean might, was not created in Mycenae or Argos or even Pylos but may have originated in some small rural place across the "wine-dark sea," neighboring the realm of old Priam.

7. LCL 496, pp. 355 ff.

8. A non infrequent, embellishing, uplifting disguise for an illegitimate pregnancy...

9. Lucian, in his fabulous *True History*, makes him out to be a Babylonian called Tigranes, who assumed the name Homer only when taken hostage by the Greeks.

10. "On that occasion, because they had lost their way, they . . . set upon the lively city of Teuthras, and there, snorting fury along with their horses, came in distress of spirit. For they thought they were attacking the high-gated city of Troy, but in fact they had their feet on wheat-bearing Mysia" (Papyrus Oxy. LXIX 4708, verses by Archilochus).

11. The Cypria LCL #57, p. 493. This tale is never addressed in the *Iliad* by Homer, unless in a very oblique fashion when he has Helen state "for this is now the twentieth year from the time when I went from there and have been gone from my native land" (*Iliad*, Book XXIV, ll. 775-776). The statement indicates, though, that Homer knew that the Trojan saga had at least a 20 year history. In a way, this version also appears to be a structural draft of the *Iliad*: a city attacked by vastly superior Achaean forces but undefeated until its hero warrior, Telephus, is taken down by Achilles, with the same Pelian spear. This time the spear did not kill, but caused a festering unhealable wound with agonizing pain (the tale also discloses that, in exchange for being healed, Telephus revealed to Achilles the correct location of Troy!).

12. "Subsequently Attarssiya, the man of Ahhiya, came and plotted to kill you, Madduwatta. But when the father of My Sun heard of this, he dispatched Kisnapili, troops and chariots, to do battle . . ." "The Indictment of Madduwatta" (ca. 1350 BC) § obv. 60-2. From: Hittite Diplomatic Texts, pp. 153 ff. ("My Sun" was the standard appellative of the Hittite Emperors).

13. "and you, my brother, have [taken(?)] 7,000 civilian captives from me. . . . Return them to me . . ." The Tawagalawa letter, archives of Hattusa: from a Hittite Great King (Muwatalli II or Hattusili III?) to a king of Ahhiyawa (Achaia); perhaps the Mycenaean Atreus or his son Agamemnon? Beckman, Bryce, Cline HiT4 (p. 113).

14. The dialect that was used for the *Iliad* is considered Asiatic Greek: a literary amalgam of Aeolic and other ancient Greek dialects, specifically Ionic (from Ionia, the Greek denomination of the Seha River territories); another indication of where Homer may have been born and was raised. This composite dialect has also been called Homeric Greek.

15. Syllabic Linear B descended from the older Linear A, an undeciphered earlier script used for writing the Minoan language. Linear B tablets were found mainly in ancient palatial archives, as in Mycenae, Thebes and Pylos.

16. Janko R. *Homer, Hesiod and the Hymns*, 1982.

17. Janko R. "Intellectual Biography and Current Research." From his homepage, public domain.

18. Venetus A is the oldest (tenth century AD), best texted, and most famous manuscript of the *Iliad*. It contains, among other material, a full text of the *Iliad* in ancient Greek; marginal critical marks shown to reflect fairly accurately those that would have been in the Alexandria scholar Aristarchus' edition of the *Iliad*; a set of marginal annotations (or scholia) derived largely from the work of Aristarchus; and summaries of all the works of the Epic Cycle except the Cypria. Venetus B It is the second oldest surviving manuscript of *the* Iliad written in the eleventh century and contains an important body of scholia.

19. Prof. M. Haslam in his paper on Homeric papyri and the transmission of the Homeric text (A New Companion to Homer, pp. 55 ff.) debates that the present text as we know it, the vulgate, was overall established by the Alexandrians, Aristarchus in particular.

20. In the introduction to his translation of the Iliad A. Pope had some comments on the need to respect the spirit of the time: "To form correct views of individuals we must regard them as forming parts of a great whole—we must measure them by their relation to the mass of beings by whom they are surrounded." He also addressed some

aspects of revisionism: "It has been an easy, and a popular expedient, of late years, to deny the personal or real existence of men and things whose life and condition were too much for our belief . . ." And added: "Skepticism has attained its culminating point with respect to Homer, and the state of our Homeric knowledge may be described as a free permission to believe any theory, provided we throw overboard all written tradition, concerning the author or authors of the *Iliad* and the *Odyssey*. What few authorities exist on the subject, are summarily dismissed. . . . It is, however, unfortunate that the professed biographies of Homer are partly forgeries, partly freaks of ingenuity and imagination, in which truth is the requisite most wanting."

21. Homer hints only once to the existence of some sort of writing, during Glaukos recounting the arrival of Bellerophon in Lycia: ". . . he sent him to Lycia, and gave him fatal tokens, scratching in a folded tablet signs many and deadly" *Iliad*, Book VI, ll. 168 ff. The description suggests some form of semasiography (sign-writing), or perhaps even a logographic message, rather than alphabetical writing.

22. Scholarly Neoanalysts support the claim that Homer drew on the legendary material which later crystallized into the Epic Cycle (other Neoanalysts claim that the cycle already existed in its complete form by the time Homer came around, and that he used it extensively).

23. Even at chronologically later dates than the beginning of the first millennium BC, the level of scribal literacy in ancient Greece was quite limited. Prof. W.V. Harris concluded that "there is no epigraphical or literary evidence to suggest that more than a small percentage of Greeks were literate before 600 BC." (Ancient Literacy, Cambridge, Mass., 1989, p. 49).

24. The first Confederacy of the Anatolian seaboard states, the Assuwan Confederacy, had already been badly beaten by the Hittite Emperor Tudhaliya I (ca. 1400 BC), when the Confederate Nations that were chasing the Hittite army on its way to Hattusa, planning to rescue the thousands of their enslaved countrymen but unaccustomed to organized campaigns and shared leaderships, failed to realize that a victorious and battle-tested emperor would not stay chased for long. Tudhaliya turned back under the cover of night, surprised the bivouacking confederate forces and piled up more slaves, including the "lords of the chariots", the noble mounted regiments of the Assuwan forces. The kingdoms, though, had survived, maintaining their dialects, customs, and deities, which they shared with the enemy. This time the outcome from Troy falling was different. Strangers from far-away places came to claim forcefully the lands; and the old dialects, customs, and deities became captive and obsolete.

25. *A New Companion to Homer*, pp. 146 ff.

26. Ibid., p. 150, (emphasis mine). The statement offers a compelling description of the psychodynamic evolution of young Homer's mind, the why's and the how's, well beyond a static analysis of what the final product was.

27. Ibid., p. 151

28. He claims that Homer was born 622 years before Xerxes I invaded Greece (480 BC); in other words, in 1102 BC!

29. Diodorus comments in his History that "in our own time . . . not a few men live over one hundred years." (I, 26).

30. The skeptical reader should reflect on how permissive the Spanish Conquistadores of the Catholic Queen Isabella were—in the second half of the sixteenth century AD!—in allowing the Incas to celebrate and glorify the history of their ancestors.

31. Thucydides, Book V, 116.

32. Ibid., pp. 599–630.

33. Ibid., p. 599.

TWO

The Epic and Its Coming to Life

Homer sets his story during fifty-one summer days of the tenth and last year of the war. More precisely, the events described in the twenty-four books happened during eleven days. The *Iliad* dismisses with thirty-one lines of text all that happened in the remaining forty days, as the plague (eight days, I, 44–52); Zeus in Ethiopia (eleven days, I, 423–424, 493); the defiling of Hector (twelve days, XXIV: 13–30); the gathering of the wood for Hector's pyre (nine days, XXIV: 782–784).

One cannot stop from wondering what the pivotal event of those eleven days was: the event and premise for which and around which Homer built the entire epic. Possibly the central and guiding inspiration had to do with something that ran under the overt theme of the wrath of Achilles, and conditioned the inevitable outcome and the subsequent fate of the whole region.[1] The remaining events of the conflagration, although majestic for the times, were overall of lesser importance, as was the case of the battle of the gods! They were all remarkable, fundamental fillings for a great tale, rich in actions and awe, worth declaiming at the courts of the powerful Greek lords, and to audiences all over; a very valued rhapsode like Homer knew the importance of being quite familiar with the origins and the main sequences of the great Greek families, and with their divine and human genealogies, in order to recall in his songs, to those local audiences, the glories of the long lines of his host's ancestors and the important role that they played in the history of the city and the region.[2] He displays this familiarity quite frequently, starting with the complete catalog of the kings and leaders who sailed to Troy, and by repeatedly accompanying duels and encounters with the genealogy of the subjects.

However, while several among these events would profoundly, and permanently, affect many destinies, they would not change history and leave an enduring memory, collectively shared through generations.

One, possibly two, events changed the course of near eastern history, at least for the minds of Homer's age: the death of Hector and that of the Lycian king Sarpedon: the two main heroes on the Trojan side, representatives of two kingdoms geographically quite distant from each other but that contained between them the spirit, the culture, and the destiny of the entire Anatolian seaboard. With their deaths the fate of the first major conflagration between Europe and Asia is sealed and unimpeded Greek colonies quickly disseminate the coast of the eastern Aegean Sea.[3]

A significant body of scholarly literature documents the in-depth studies of Homer's work that have been conducted through the centuries, either in the form of translations, or as critical analyses of its historical value and of the persistent significance of its rich content (the great majority of these studies are linked by a shared western collective sociocultural milieu). An example of such interpretive works is the book "Achilles in Vietnam" by Dr. J. Shay, in which the author, with significant insight and level of experience, connects the behavior of Achilles in Books XX–XXII to the dynamics of post-traumatic stress disorder (PTSD) and to the berserk state among Vietnam veterans, pointing to battle grief and to survivors' guilt as the commonly shared determinants in both instances.

However, I want to repeat once more that during the reading of all these studies consideration should be also given to the influence of the sociocultural milieu specific to their authors; one should be aware of the inevitable differences between those systems and what may have been the "psychic system"[4] of Homer, as his young mind gradually absorbed and processed information, on his way to compose the epic, and how that mind came to conceptualize its content; and the modern reader should look for proof that the authors were cognizant of those differences and elaborated them in their works.

Prof. Frank Turner, in his essay on the Homeric Question,[5] which he defines as "a distinctly nineteenth-century invention," explored the contamination that it caused to the reading of Homer, in that "philologists wrested Homer from the world of poets and literature and placed him at the mercy of modern scientific criticism, just as they wrested the Christian scriptures from the realm of sacred reverence." He then continued: "To grasp Homer in all his fullness required that the imagination escape to a different time and place. Blackwell, for example, had argued that readers must set themselves into the audience of ancient warriors who understood all of the customs that Homer's verse described and recounted."[6]

Blackwell was referring to an audience appropriate for the warring aspect of the *Iliad*, but the concept would equally apply to present readers, who need to set themselves into a broadened audience of those ancient populations in order to better understand the entirety and depth of the tragedy played at Troy.

My attention to the complexity of the interaction among these three psychodynamic systems—the classical Greek vision of the world and of Greece's primacy; the "spirit of the time" of the western Anatolian Bronze Age kingdoms; and the modern Western sociocultural milieu—was enhanced by reading the stimulating book *The War That Killed Achilles* by Dr. Caroline Alexander.

The story of how this book came to life is truly captivating. A participant to the current western collective psyche, as a fourteen-year-old adolescent Ms. Alexander was entranced by Lattimore's poetic translation of the *Iliad* and by the figure of Achilles. The appeal of the poem and of her favorite hero moved her to learn Classical Greek, in order to be able and read the saga in its original language, on her way to become a Rhodes Scholar and Marion Fellow in Humanities at Columbia University. In an endearing indication of where her psychic system ultimately rests on this subject, her description of the *Iliad* and its events follows closely the text of Lattimore; however, for book XXII (the duel between Achilles and Hector, the death of Hector, and his parents' grief) she abandons Lattimore and prefers to rely on her own translation.

I was, as she was, a product of the Western collective psyche when, in my very early teens—younger even than Dr. Alexander—I read for the first time the *Iliad* and became quite taken by it, by the famous hero Achilles, and by the mythical figure of that old, blind author. I went through a phase during which I kept drawing phalanxes of Greek (Myrmidon!) warriors, spears pointing forward, hidden behind their plumed helms and their shields, following their invulnerable Commander. I could not escape, I was not even aware that I could not escape, my cultural heritage, with a family imbedded in it for generations, and an idealized great-grandfather who spoke fluent Greek and Latin, and was a published scholar in old Etruscan writings and history.[7] As was the case for Dr. Alexander, my first *Iliad* was also a beautiful poetic Italian translation (with accompanying Greek text) of the Homeric work.[8] Later on, my preference shifted, though, to literal translations, my favorite being the one by A.T. Murray (revised by his grandnephew W.F. Wyatt).[9] The change was motivated by my consideration that the main objective for a literal translator is to produce a text that would be as faithful as possible to the original Greek version; while poetic translators see their work as a statement not only of their mastery in the language of Homer but also, and significantly, of their skills as epic poets; in these last types of versions, a strictly literal translation had to be subjected to poetic adaptation; and poetry is significantly more susceptible to the current expectations and sociocultural guidelines than a literal translation of an ancient text would be. Telling examples of the impact of collective psychological forces (the spirit of the time) upon the rendering of ancient material were the exclusions, by Aristarchus, of lines 29–31 in Book I, possibly to reject the cruel words of Agamemnon; and of lines 458–461 in Book IX, as

Aristarchus was reportedly terrified by the idea of parricide. This last omission continued in most ancient manuscripts, until the lines were rediscovered in the writings of Plutarch (*Moralia*, 26, f.).

Another great example of poetical rearrangement of the *Iliad* is the one by Fitzgerald, used by Dr. Shay, which distinctly shows the amount of degrees of freedom from the Greek text as compared to literal translations like the one from Murray. Shay had to work out a corrective mathematical formula in order for the reader to locate his verse quotations in the original.[10] Such levels of poetic license—compounded by the affective spirit of the time directing the creative process of translators-poets like Fitzgerald and suggesting the styles preferred by their specific epochs—need to be kept in mind during the analytical investigation of Homer's mental landscapes. This caveat is even more crucial when the analytical focus is centered on the affective coordinate rather than the descriptive one: on Eros rather than Logos.[11]

Dr. Caroline and I are examples of how a life-long passion evolves through a progressive journey from its adolescent roots to its educated fulfillment. It is very rare for an "Iliad" to sprout, completed, out of an adult mind, the like of an Athene from the head of Zeus. Even then, a psychodynamic analysis usually discloses its previously unrecognized, potent, emotionally charged antecedents. A similar, and even more fascinating path is the one followed by Prof. R. Janko and described in his intellectual biography; a path that started with a reading of the *Odyssey* at age seven and brought him to a distinguished professorship in Classical Studies at the University of Michigan!

My reading of how Dr. Alexander's passionate commitment to a specific Iliad and its special hero unfolded in her mind, together with the resurfacing memories of a similar process shaping similar images in my mind—both sets of events pointing to a shared psychic system—eventually stirred my curiosity in Homer's mental landscape and in the psychodynamics out of which his *Iliad* emerged.

I became also disturbed, in my western passion for the *Iliad* and the grandeur of the Grecian heroes, by the subtle yet nagging feeling of an affective dissonance, while reading the Epic, in the way Homer deals with the Achaean theme and the Trojan theme. Something appeared amiss, hidden under the overt saga of Greek conquest. Consequently, this hidden subtext became a main focus of the present analysis.

One can presume that the composition of the *Iliad* gradually took form along a path similar to that of Dr. Alexander and mine; a path that characterizes the progressive elaboration and consolidation of any major commitment to a truly life-long task: from disjointed but cathexis-laden fragments that activate the imagination of the child, and then of the adolescent, to their coalescing into a complex unifying gestalt.[12] I became intrigued in attaining some understanding of his psychic configuration, its formative forerunners and its orientation, as free as possible from any contaminating countertransference of mine, in consonance with the basic design of all psychotherapeutic journeys.

Concerning the background of the *Iliad*, when Homer grew up information and knowledge were largely distributed, and passed on through generations, by word of mouth as the storyteller, or the bard, or the rhapsode. It is also probable, if we stay with the dating of Pseudo Herodotus, and still possible even if we follow the estimates of Herodotus and of Janko, that during his childhood Homer may have heard reports of the Trojan War and of the Seha River lands of old—spreading all the way up to the Troad from the immortalized Karabel Pass with the greater-than-life effigy of King Tarkasnawa of Mira carved in the stone[13]—narrated by some elder who had heard them, as a child, from some other elder who, if not himself a witness, had heard of the fall of the city—and of the demise of the kingdom—from someone who had lived through those momentous events.

The very young Homer certainly cherished the tellers and their stories, and he would hear descriptions of the land and its heroes even among tales arriving from far-away places—from Hattusa to Carchemish to distant Achaia. Concurrently, he would hear about other great and inspiring heroes and other mighty cities and kingdoms across the sea, powerfully firing up the mind of the youngster surrounded by the life of a fishermen island like Chios or the subdued rural milieu of Old Smyrna.[14]

Some of those stories, more than others, may have deeply captured his imagination, as Achilles and Book XXII captured the imagination of Dr. Alexander, while the Myrmidons withdrawal and the fatidic duel captured mine. His creativity used these stories to begin and weave what would become the intricate and complex tapestry of his *Iliad*.

A task of such magnitude requires serious and prolonged work to retrieve and organize the material that will inspire and constitute the finished product. In her compelling journey Dr. Alexander had to learn at great depth the Greek language in order to have direct access to Homer's description of the events of that summer and of the role of her hero. The complexity and the length of the journey speaks to the intensity and power of her inspiration and of her commitment.

Homer most likely had no problems with the Greek language; he had been exposed to its local version since infancy. His problem was to collect all the available elements for his story: a story charged with competing themes, meanings, and affective valences. As he grew up, he most likely added to the fragments from local storytelling, and from the information percolating through generations of elderlies, the material available from the Epic Cycle.

As already mentioned, the cyclic epics survive only in fragments and summaries. All of them were related to the story of the Trojan War. The Cypria dealt with the Judgement of Paris and with the events leading up to the war and the first nine years of the conflict. The Aethiopis described the arrival of the Trojan allies after the death of Hector, the Amazons and their Queen Penthesileia, and the Ethiopian King Memnon; their deaths at Achilles' hands; and Achilles' own death. The Little Iliad allegedly covered the events after Achilles' death, including the building of the Trojan horse. The Iliupersis was centered on the destruction of Troy. The Nostoi dealt with the return home of the Greek force, including Agamemnon and Menelaus; while the theme of the Telegony was another journey of Odysseus to Theosprotia, his return from there to Ithaca, and his death at the hands of the illegitimate son Telegonus.

The sheer number of these works centered on the Trojan events strongly speaks to the richness and vibrancy of the entire Trojan saga, from which all of them had been inspired, and to the level and type of mental stimuli that moved the imagination of those ancient pre-literal audiences, to whom information and entertainment were presented, most often during the same settings, by all sorts of storytellers and rhapsodes; and Homer would have certainly sat among the crowd, from a very young age. His enchantment with the material, and the sharing of those feelings with a world still very connected to that history, would unquestionably have been much greater than the enchantment of Dr. Alexander, or Prof. Janko, or mine!

Homer certainly went to visit the theater of his epic. The less than 300 miles that separated Smyrna from the ruins of Troy were surely no impediment. While on the way he most likely visited also the remnants of Lyrnessus; the raid of the place by Achilles had provided the foundation for the opening of the *Iliad*: it produced the two women, Briseis and Chryseis, who became the unwilling sources of high dramas in the Greek camp, as I will revisit later on. He walked through the ruins of the lower city, not yet totally obliterated by the great changes in the topography of the plain that will eventually erase any sign of its existence.[15] Indeed, the Troy of Laomedon and Priam had been one of the largest, heavily fortified[16] sites of the Bronze Age, with the lower city adding ca. 0.10 mls^2 to the 0.01 mls^2 of the citadel of Ilium, and a population of several thousand people. Located on an important trade route from the Orient, Troy had been the capital of a large kingdom that was significantly greater than any Greek counterpart; its boundaries span from the "briny" waters of the Aegean and Hellespontine seas to the dark waters of the Aisepos River, all the way down to sacred Mount Ida and the Adramyttian shores; "its circumference...includes about five hundred English miles."[17] Its capital was a major center that could compare even with the contemporary Hittite capital of Hattusa.[18]

I mentioned earlier how as a child Homer had grown up in a primarily rural area of petty centers that appear from their archeological remains to have been at best poorly fortified villages, the remnants of those older and vigorous systems that had been plundered and devastated by ten years of war; he seems to have been deeply affected by the early experiences of walking along the vestiges of such an imposing city as Troy had been. The deep impression that the city left on him, and his careful attention to its surroundings are demonstrated by his knowledge of the local topography and by the repeated descriptions of Troy (the lower city) as broad, well lived, well built, with wide streets, strong walls with beautiful towers and high doors; while he preferentially describes Ilium (the acropolis) as steep, windy, and primarily sacred or holy (he used this last definition at least two dozen times).

It would be a major error, contaminated by projective material from our collective sociocultural basin, to try to specify the affective valence that Homer's mind assigned to those early images. We can only infer, by looking at the completed project, the existence of sets of primary images gravid with inspirational feeling that provided for the highly charged psychological dynamic factors at the root of, and supplying ongoing energy to, the entire creative process.

The psyche of young Homer may have been enchanted and captivated by Greek might and heroes, either as a part of his heritage as a Greek citizen by Greek parents, or, if not Greek, by a mechanism of identification with the oppressor, which allowed him to vicariously incorporate the grandeur of Greece, and to find in the shadow of her exceptional heroes, as an Achilles, a sense of self-repairing aggrandizement. In this sense he may have responded to the collective innate need for essentialism[19] that was brewing among some aspects of the local population, out of the desire to belong, not to be perceived and to perceive themselves (in a psychic sense this being a most important affective dimension), as "They" rather than "We" in the face of the ongoing Greek expansionism; to recreate a spurious protective feeling of group identity, which had dissipated during the process of invasion and colonization.

Concurrently, the child from local parents shared deeply of the surrounding collective grief for the tragedy that had been played out at Troy, where the ancestors of the people joined a coalition to battle for a decade an immense invasion, and for the idealized heroes who fought against forces vastly superior until they also fell, cut down by the decision of unrelenting gods; while the Greek child, instead, may have responded to a process of identification with the victimized and the vulnerable, with the tragic hero felled while trying to protect the woman (mother/lover) from stronger rivals.[20]

From a psychodynamic perspective, in the case of Homer we may expect that the psyche of the child most likely figured out a path, and a landscape, that would provide both configurations just described with their mental space and with a way to manifest themselves, side by side, either through descriptively clear, explicit images or in more subdued, implicit ways. He could in this manner placate to some extent the tension between conflicting opposites, respond to a need to integrate, to make some sense out of all that sequence of evocative images and capturing narratives that kept flooding his imagination, charged with forceful and often deeply contrasting emotional valences.

An effective and successful analysis requires that detailed, significant, recurrent attention (and time!) be repeatedly given to statements and to single words: sensitive to what is said as well as (and perhaps more) to what is not said, what should probably have been indicated and appropriate for the content of the observable theme but was not expressed due to some operative defensive mechanism; or to what appears to be idiosyncratic or incongruent with that theme. These oddities in the logical constructs reveal the presence of nonverbal, emotionally driven variables acting as attractors embedded within the phase-space[21] of the construct, and their effect upon the cognitive organization of the material. The analytical process requires also a careful observation and exploration of the link—or lack thereof—between the cognitive discourse and its affective counterpart. It eventually requires the identification of "affect linking"[22] between distant and or apparently unrelated cognitive constructs: the emotional link that reveals an analogical connectedness, in that both constructs represent different metaphors of the same affective experience.[23]

An analysis of the affective tapestry of the *Iliad* that runs its course intertwined with the cognitive tapestry[24] may bring into greater evidence, offer greater appreciation for, Homer's "movement of the heart" and his instinctive emotional positioning toward the Greek and the Trojan landscapes. In other words, the focus on my analysis will be on the search for an affective resonance, if any is there to be found, to the cognitive discourse of the *Iliad*: when did the poet become absorbed by the domain of feelings, of the instinctive and the essential, the obscure side of psyche, with sufficient cathexis for the affect to percolate through the cognitive aspects of the ego: the domains of the descriptive and of the manifest; and what were the valence and the arousal level of that cathectic load.[25]

Therefore, while conducting a psychodynamic analysis of the *Iliad* we have to silence the feelings that the reading of the epic elicits in us—and which represent the summation of our personal and sociocultural Zeitgeist—and give exclusive attention to the feelings that Homer felt and that provided the compelling cathexis—or allocation of positive emotional charge—to his creation.

I will work on a reconstruction of Homer's mind by analyzing the available information concerning three areas of affective significance: Homer's standing regarding the wrath of Achilles, from the initial strife with Agamemnon to its evolution through time; his feelings and his overt or covert judgement about the gods and the Greek and Trojan relationship to them (devotion and reverence, piety and impiety); and his expressions of genuine—rather than formulaic[26]—empathy for specific characters and situations, as well as hints of a more personal nature.

The analysis will operate on the relationship between the language spoken and the person who did the speaking, to the extent that I could reconstruct the figure of Homer out of the available information from different sources. As I already mentioned when I described my search of the progressive development for the main Iliadic narratives, I readily admit that in the reconstruction of this figure I once more preferred to rely on sources as chronologically close to him as possible; fully aware of the distortions originating from the many variables—personal and social—that may have affected those sources, but also aware that similar powerful variables, born out of the chronological distance and of the imposing sociocultural changes that evolved through the past two or three millennia, have posed an equally heavy weight upon later scholastic studies. These studies could not possibly <u>feel</u> the familiarity to Homeric ways of daily living and culture as they were perceived by a Hesiod or other historians who had been at the most a few generations removed from Homer, and had all shared of the Hellenistic milieu that prevailed along the Mediterranean basin.

NOTES

1. The term Ἰλιάς (Ilias) is the elliptic for ἡ ποίησις Ἰλιάς (he poíesis Iliás), meaning "the Trojan Poem." From a Greek/Western perspective its implicit given meaning is of a poem about the war at Troy, the city; but for the populations of the Anatolian seaboard it could instead have meant a poem about the vast kingdom of Troy and the Trojan people; in Book XXIV, Priam will remind Achilles that Hector "fought for his country." The poem therefore may be inspired by a momentous event in the history of the region, rather than simply about a city target of a destructive war.

2. The significant advantage from knowing how to gratify Greek audiences is well illustrated in the following report: "The Argive officials were exceedingly delighted to hear their race being praised by the most celebrated of poets. They honored him with costly gifts, set up a bronze statue of him..." *Lives of Homer* LCL 496 p. 349.

3. There has to be a special motive that inspired Homer to make such a hero of Sarpedon and prefer him to the several other kings and leaders from places closer to Troy than distant Lykia. He depicted the Lykian king as the fiercest warrior among the Trojan allies, the one who rebuked Hector in more than one occasion but also fought at his side and took down the defensive Greek wall; the son of Zeus who ultimately fell by the spear of Patroclus.

4. By psychic system I mean the interactive complex of an individual psyche and its collective spiritual, cultural, and social counterparts.

5. *A New Companion to Homer*, p. 123 ff.

6. Ibid., p. 124.

7. I am an example of the impact that an idealized figure, three generations removed, can have on the mind of a child. Who were Homer's idealized figures of old, whose messages about the Trojan events were certainly significantly more numinous than those of my great-grandfather?

8. *Iliade*. (Translation of. Rosa Calzecchi Onesti) Einaudi, Torino, 1950.

9. Homer, *Iliad* (Transl. A.T. Murray) Loeb Classical Library, Harvard University Press, 1999.

10. Shay, p. 211, note # 2.

11. An instance of the risks from poetic interpretations is the translation reported by Shay (p. 85) of the term λύθρον as mire, intended as "feces let go by the terrified Trojans " rather than the usually recognized blood mixed with dust (gore). The point here is not whether by λύθρον Homer meant gore or mire (he actually meant gore, given that a few lines earlier he mentions twice blood splattering everything and darkening the earth), but rather what moved Fitzgerald (and Shay) to chose one translation rather than the other and to propose a Trojan ownership of the λύθρον, rather than an Achaean, or equine, or combination thereof. Consideration is also requested for the impact of the length of the war upon the present description: soldiers seasoned by years of war at Troy (or in Vietnam), may have learned to scatter quickly in front of a war chariot (or an incoming tank) without necessarily defecating during the process. The affective valence and arousal values operating in the mind of Fitzgerald (and Shay) seem rather indicative of his overall orientation about the two opposing camps and of the potential interpretive bias pervading his entire opus. (Homer uses the same term for Agamemnon in Book XI, l. 169, as well as for Hector in Book VI, l.268.). This prolonged footnote is an example of the level of detailed attention required by an appropriate in-depth psychological analysis of the affective contents hidden behind the manifest cognitive ones.

12. Hesychius of Miletus was of the idea that Homer composed separately each of the rhapsodies that eventually were put together by Zenodotus, and performed them "as he went round from town to town to make a living" (*Lives of Homer*, LCL # 496, p. 429).

13. From Hittite diplomatic letters it is known that the Seha river region was bordered on one side by the kingdom of Mira and on the other side by Wilusa, as the kingdom of Troy (ilium) was known to the Hittites.

14. Old Smyrna was probably founded on a small peninsula by indigenous people around the end of the second millennium BC; it rose to prominence as one of the principal ancient Greek settlements in western Anatolia during the Greek Archaic Period, from the eighth century to the beginning of the fifth century BC, until its residents moved to the new, flourishing Smyrna of Alexander the Great in the fourth century BC. Its major development was posterior to Homer's times, and even more so for Chios, under local rulers until it fell, too, under Greek influence and entered the Ionian league in the eighth century BC.

15. Located as it was at the edge of the alluvial plain of two rivers—the Scamander and the Simois—three millennia of accumulated silt (J.C. Kraft, G. Rapp, I. Kayan, and J.V. Luce) and scavenging by builders profoundly affected the site of the lower city. Already Lucan at the very beginning of the present era had mentioned that "its very ruins were annihilated" (Pharsalia, Book 9, v. 969).

16. The surveys conducted since 1992 by Hans Gunter Jansen, a physicist and expert on geomagnetic surveying, under Manfred Korfmann's direction, suggested evidence for a wide ditch cut into the bedrock. The trench probably served as the first line of defense. A high wall stood inside the line of the trench, but its stones were long ago removed and reused for the fortifications of the Sigeum (Strabo 13, I, 38) and for the Greco-Roman Novum Ilium.

17. R. Wood, p. 311.

18. Even Achilles reminds Priam of the extent of his kingdom Book XXIV, ll. 543 ff.

19. Philosopher and social theorist Kwame Anthony Appiah [Appiah K.A. (2015) *Race in the Modern World*. Foreign Affairs, v. 95 (2)] defines essentialism as the universal need for human groups to have strong core properties in common (properties that would make all their members essentially the same), and as the universal inclination for humans to attribute deep commonalities (physical, geographical, religious) to alike-looking people (people who look alike are also intrinsically alike and share essentially the same value systems). Essentialism, therefore, is the primary component of the boundary between the "We" and the "They." When conceptualized from this perspective, essentialism assumes the qualities of an archetype, a powerful collective organizing template for social relatedness and behavior. [See also Sanguineti VS: "The

roles of essentialism and religion as scaffolds to terrorism: some psychohistorical considerations," In *Before and After Violence*. Lexington Books, (2018) Ed. S. Akhtar, p. 57 ff.]

20. "... fighting with warriors for their women's sake." Achilles describes in this way what he did most during the past nine years. *Iliad*, Book IX, l. 327.

21. In non-linear classical science (A. Scott) an attractor is a condition that imposes a specific directional weight to the dynamic process, a constraint upon selected neuronal assemblies of the cognitive hierarchy. Phase-space of a mental event defines a space that contains all the possible variables that participate to the ultimate definition of the outcome. (See also Sanguineti, *The Rosetta Stone*, p. 15 ff.)

22. Yale Prof. in computer science D. Gelernter, in his book *The Muse in the Machine* defines affect linking as the connection between very separate cognitive events that include the same emotional palette. He states that the phenomenon requires the psychic apparatus to operate at the low-focus end of the cognitive thinking spectrum, and that for affect linking to happen the thinker must experience, "feel," the events. (p. 28 ff.)

23. Prof. G. Edelman (Nobel prize in neurophysiology and profound scholar of consciousness), in one of his latest works—aptly titled "Wider than the sky" in reference to E. Dickinson's poem—comments that "while logic can prove theorems ... it cannot chose axioms." And, again, "the products of metaphorical abilities, while necessarily ambiguous, can be richly creative. Logic is not creative." He concluded with a metaphor of his own: "selectionism is the mistress of our thoughts, while logic is their housekeeper."

24. Similar to most great creative works, the structure of the *Iliad* contains both a figurative, objectively discernible and shared external dimension and an internal, affective, primarily evocative one, of problematic articulation and of uncertain, predominantly intersubjective recognition and identification.

25. Prof. A. Kaszniak researched in depth specific conscious and unconscious aspects of positive and negative emotions. He explored how these concepts might illustrate the search for homeostasis that could represent the core function of affectivity. The research suggested that the subjective experience of emotions is guided, among other factors, by a valence dimension and an arousal dimension. The valence dimension indicates the pleasure-displeasure weight that the brain allocates to a specific stimulus. The arousal dimension indicates the level of emotional content or experience that a stimulus has to generate in order to elicit a response. Further experimental research indicated that both arousal and valence can be subjectively experienced in the absence of conscious awareness of the stimulus.

26. As mentioned earlier on, Homer depended on a tradition of formulaic language made up of familiar, repetitive phrases, which Parry called formulas or "expression(s) regularly used, under the same metrical conditions, to express an essential idea" (Foley, p. 147). This phraseology, although metrically fitting the poetic text, did not belong to the true poetic language that Homer used to sing his great story; therefore it does not convey any affective message of significance.

THREE
Homer and the Greeks

BOOK I: A DESCRIPTIVE ANALYSIS

I will start with a very detailed, purely descriptive analysis of the "presenting complaint," the equivalent of an initial therapeutic encounter: the content of the *Iliad*'s opening scenes in Book I. As is often the case, the opening lines have special importance: they represent the first concrete step toward the transformation of the highly cathected idea into a representational object; the mental content begins to assume a form, to define the path through which its libidinal charge will find its organized expression and its satisfaction.[1] The moment came when the imagination of young Homer had been sufficiently enriched and was ready to become alive; he had reached an adequate outline of the overall structure of his work, and how to convey its central themes around and upon which the entire epic will be gradually constructed. These themes were the most pressing and came to life immediately; they infiltrated and colored the creative landscape from the very first verses, either explicitly or implicitly. A dynamic analysis looking for the meanings imbedded in the data will follow the descriptive one, with the identification and recognition of patterns giving depth and life to the presenting material.

Homer opens the *Iliad* with two demands. He starts by asking the Goddess to sing about the accursed, destructive wrath of Achilles,[2] and the moment when he and Agamemnon parted in strife; and then proceeds with his second demand: "Who of the gods was it who brought these two together to contend?"[3]

The scene then shifts immediately to the Achaean camp. Chryses, a Trojan priest of Apollo at the god's temple a short distance southwest of Troy, comes to the camp of the Greek army, showing the insignia of his priesthood, to ransom his daughter Chryseis, a spoil of war in the hands (and to the bed) of Atreides Agamemnon; the army "shouted their agreement, to respect the priest and accept the glorious ransom" but Agamemnon does not agree. He plans to keep his prize Chryseis with him, to share his house and his bed through old age. He befouls the priest's insignia and threatens him with a severe beating or worse, should he try to return with his demand.[4]

Chryses leaves but prays his god for revenge, and Apollo for nine days rains his arrows on the Greek camp, indiscriminately killing animals and men. The son of Peleus, Achilles, calls an assembly of the army, to find a reason for the plague, and Calchas the diviner reveals the impiety.[5]

After having been accused, Agamemnon becomes enraged and invests the seer Calchas with harsh, rage-filled words: "Prophet of evil, never yet have you given me a favorable prophesy; always it is dear to your heart to prophesy evil."[6]

Agamemnon then describes how important Chryseis is to him, preferring her to his wife; however, for the sake of the entire army, he agrees to return Chryseis to her father. He demands, though, adequate remuneration, given that he is doing it for the good of them all in order to "rather have the army safe than perishing." He points out that it would be unfair for him to go without a prize, because as everyone can see, his prize "goes from me elsewhere."[7]

Achilles is the first—and only one—to respond. His initial response is discreet in its content, although his language is already confrontational. He addresses Agamemnon as "most covetous,"[8] but he also invites the Commander-in-Chief to wait for the retribution until Troy falls; then the Greeks "will recompense you threefold and fourfold, if ever Zeus grants us to sack the well-walled city of Troy."[9]

The proposal, as formulated by Homer through the words of Achilles, does not sit well with Agamemnon. Not only he has to give up his prize, a primary symbol of his honor, in order to benefit the entire army and the other kings; he is also asked to wait for recompense until Troy falls: a dubious event at best, after nine unsuccessful years of fighting and the plan to return home before winter sets in, irrespective of the outcome of the war. He responds that he has heard Achilles' demand to return Chryseis,[10] but does not see how Pelides can ask him to be the only one, in the entire army, to suffer from the loss of his prize, and honor. He demands the "great-hearted" Achaeans to give him as a recompense a prize of equivalent value; otherwise he will take one of his choice from either Achilles, or Aias, or Odysseus. Still, he tries to mollify Achilles by suggesting that "you, son of Peleus, of all men most daunting," should lead the delegation that will bring Chryseis back, offer sacrifice, and appease the god Apollo "who works from afar."

At this Achilles explodes, although Agamemnon has not yet decided where he will turn to get the payback for his loss, but has simply listed a series of options. The son of Peleus escalates the confrontation to a totally new level; he addresses Agamemnon with a series of debasing and foul epithets, like "dog-face" and "clothed in shamelessness . . . how can any Achaean eagerly obey your words either to go on a journey or to do battle"[11]; and he accompanies his vilification with a threat to leave the alliance and return home.

Agamemnon is left little choice, if he wants to save face in front of the army; he answers that Achilles may leave anytime for "most hateful to me are you of the kings, nurtured by Zeus, for always is strife dear to you, and wars and battle." With Agamemnon are "others that will do me honor, and above all Zeus, the lord of counsel."[12] Before leaving, though, Achilles will have to give fair-cheeked Briseis to Agamemnon, "so that you may well know how much mightier I am than you, and another too may shrink from declaring himself my equal and likening himself to me in my face."[13]

Achilles' rage reaches a murderous level, requiring the intervention of Athene to stop him from trying to kill Agamemnon. The goddess, in the name of Hera, asks him to "cease from strife . . . with words indeed taunt him . . . one day three times as many glorious gifts will be yours on account of this insult."[14] Achilles tells her he will obey both goddesses but he does not cease his wrath, and his language is so full of insults that Zenodotus rejected nine lines of text as possibly too defamatory of both characters.[15] He will ultimately withdraw his Myrmidons from the alliance and will swear that he will never return to the battlefield and that the Achaeans will suffer terribly because of his withdrawal.

At this point old Nestor inserts some attempts at reconciliation, cautioning both parties to avoid rushed decisions that they would regret later on. We will return to this figure; presently he is introduced by Homer as "sweet of speech, the clear-voiced orator of the men of Pylos, he from whose tongue speech flowed sweeter than honey. Two generations of mortal men he had already seen pass away, who long ago were born and reared with him in sacred Pylos, and he was king among the third." He advises Agamemnon against taking Briseis from Achilles, and reminds Achilles that Agamemnon has been sceptered by Zeus, and Pelides should not try to contend with him equal to equal. Agamemnon agrees with the words of Nestor, but points out how Achilles wants always to be king over everyone and refuses to be told what to do. Rather than responding directly to Nestor, Achilles interrupts the Atreides and reiterates his refusal to obey anymore to Agamemnon's demands; he will not fight for Briseis because "you are only taking away what you gave,"[16] but he will fight if Agamemnon tries to take by force any other part of Achilles' bounty.

The scene then moves to the hut of Achilles where the heralds come to take away Briseis. Patroclus, who had been at the assembly, had witnessed the entire confrontation, and had accompanied Achilles back to the huts, silently obeys Achilles and delivers her to the heralds. She leaves, "all unwilling." Achilles cries, goes to sit at the seashore and calls to his mother, divine Thetis, complaining that Agamemnon "has done me dishonor, for he has taken away and holds my prize through his own arrogant act"; and he demands that she asks Zeus to punish Agamemnon and the entire army by allowing the Trojans to pen the Danaans ". . . among the sterns of their ships and around the sea as they are killed, so that they may profit of their king."[17]

Curiously, around the end of Book I, Homer inserts a pause of twelve days to the dynamics of the strife—the trip of all the gods to the feast offered by the Ethiopians "at the Ocean." It is a bit of an enigma why the poet did that. Possibly the twelve days pause is a way to establish the strife as a permanent condition rather than a passing outburst. Apparently the war went on, because Homer leaves the domain of men—and shifts his attention to the divine realm, starting with the encounter between Zeus and Thetis—with the last image we have of Achilles, until he will reappear in Book IX: full of rage, he sits "beside his swift-faring ships . . . never did he go to the place of assembly, where men win glory, nor ever to war, but allowed his heart to waste away, as he remained there; and he longed for the war cry and battle."[18]

To conclude: two key themes are presented by the tenth line of the epic: the wrath of Achilles and the relationship between Gods and humans, with its cardinal requisites of human reverence and devotion.

In addition, Book I presents us also, as already mentioned, with the figure of Nestor. In Book II he will be described as the king of Pylos and leader of the second largest contingent—ninety ships!—after that of Agamemnon and his one hundred ships. In Book VIII he will be on his chariot in the mixt of the battlefield, struggling with a dying horse, rescued at the last moment by Diomedes, planning to act as his charioteer against Hector but then, scared by Zeus' lightning, suggesting the son of Tydeus that they should desist and run away to the Greek camp instead.[19] In Book I, though, it seems that Homer introduced "the Gerenian horseman" as the personification of Greek wisdom in old age (Agamemnon will wish he had more counselors of Nestor's caliber).[20]

On a different take, Nestor had also become an orphan as a young child out of the vindictive slaying of his family by Heracles, and had survived because he had been reared in the town of Gerenia (from which comes Homer's regular label of Nestor as Gerenian). In addition, his very long age, spanning over three generations while showing him still very active and skilled in driving war chariots in the mixt of battle,[21] may be explained through the genealogy suggested by Apollodorus. In his Bibliotheca (Book III) Nestor is described as a grandson of Niobe, whom the avenging god Apollo had gifted with the lives of his slain uncles (or so a late fable reports).

BOOK 1: A DYNAMIC ANALYSIS OF THE OPENING DEMANDS

As just mentioned, the importance given by scholars of Homer to the opening statements finds its confirmation from the psychodynamic perspective, in that what is most pressing in a human mind often is presented among the first topics, either in an open or in an implicit form. Interestingly, of the two main themes—the two demands—that Homer opens the *Iliad* with, it is the first one that has received the overwhelming attention from the western scholars.

Most of them consider the theme of Achilles' wrath as the organizing element of the poem, and its significance in the context of the entire work has been repeatedly analyzed to various degrees and from various perspectives. The meaning and interpretations of the word menis (μῆνις) itself have run almost into the absurd, starting with its etymology[22]; the putatively strongest theory concluded that menis is (or hides?) a taboo word that could not be spoken aloud by the subject; therefore it was subjected to some unpredictable phonological deformation so that it could be uttered. The favorite English translation of menis as "wrath" includes some divine component to the anger. I fantasize that in Homer's mind the word was suffused with the meaning attached to the Eastern Indo-European word mainiiu of the Old Avestan hymns: the name for the twin conflicting spirits, one good and the other evil, who stand at the origin of the world, and who may reappear, as an archetypal derivative, in the Patroclus-Achilles dyad!

Dr. Alexander sees the initial quarrel as a compelling example of the effect of an incompetent generalship upon the morale of an army, with a powerful Achilles challenging an inept Agamemnon and his role as Chief of the Achaean forces. Her entire book is the progressive reinforcement of the figure of her hero as the unrivalled commander,[23] who could not possibly accept the pettiness, dishonesty, and cowardice of his Commander in Chief, while being himself driven by his status of a semi-god and by his own tragic fate.

However, since the very first lines, something is subtly confusing concerning how Homer related to Achilles. The poet has Achilles call the assembly, but then specifies that in fact it was Hera to direct him to do so.[24] Why does Homer make such a statement that reframes the ownership of such decision? Homer captures with this metaphor—another example of his rich analogical thinking—a crucial psychodynamic element behind Achilles' behavior that will resurface through several disguised images: his conflicted relationship with the feminine. Who really cares about the Achaean army is a numinous feminine psychic component, an anima manifestation of Achilles, a goddess-mother archetypal derivative, which directs the masculine hero into action.[25]

This relationship requires to be understood in the context of its antecedents and its extended psychodynamic history. His mother, the Nereid

Thetis, was forced by Zeus to marry against her will a mortal, Peleus, because an old prophecy, allegedly by Themis (as reported by Pindar in the Eighth Isthmian Ode), stated that her son would be greater than his father. Therefore, Zeus and Poseidon were concerned that she could marry a god and have a child who would dethrone them. Achilles was the obligated product of Thetis' union with a mortal. Apollonius of Rhodes recounts the entire tale in the *Argonautica*,[26] presumably out of material from the Epic Cycle, and reports that she despised Achilles' mortal condition and attempted to make him immortal by burning away his mortality in a fire at night and anointing him with ambrosia during the day.

When Peleus caught her searing the baby, he let out a cry. "Thetis heard him, and catching up the child threw him screaming to the ground, and she like a breath of wind passed swiftly from the hall as a dream and leapt into the sea, exceeding angry, and thereafter returned never again."[27] Indeed, from the *Iliad* one can construe that her relationship with Peleus had ended: Thetis lives with the other Nereids in her father's underwater realm.

This developmental background may well explain Achilles psychic splitting over the experience with the primary object: the goddess, eternal, through whom he will find the expression of his aggressive drive, as she procures both the Zeus-mandated revenge and the divine armor that will literally save him from Hector's spear thrust; and the all too human maternal figures of Phoenix and, primarily, Patroclus, nurturing and dependable but also constraining and to be sacrificed to unbound Ares. The theme is masterly played out by Homer in the elaboration of the Patroclus-Achilles dyad, as I will analyze later on.

The strife, and what it reveals about the psychological make-up of its characters, is without doubt a central aspect of the *Iliad*; Greek quarrelling and Achilles' destructive, eventually untamed aggression will continue until toward the end of the epic; they pervade it and therefore command full attention. However, as the work of Dr. Alexander indicates, most scholarly studies reflect the influence of the spirit of our time, so that less critical attention is given to what follows the first seven lines, when Homer presents a second demand: "Who of the gods was it who brought these two together to contend?"

While his first demand asks for clarification about Greek aggressive argumentation, the individual interactions, and the content of the quarrel, in the second demand Homer seeks information about a much deeper level of the strife: the relationship with the dimension of the divine, what type of suprahuman event cascaded into the human level to activate the confrontation and its devastating aftereffects upon myriads of lives. With this demand Homer immediately presents the second theme that will also run through the entire poem to its very end: the predetermined tragedy of the city and of what it represents; the complicated, demanding, capricious interaction between mortals and gods; the constant hovering of Fate at the highest level of the divine hierarchy; the expression of intense spiritual love accompanied by reverence for the gods—or lack of it—and the always-present risk from the sin of impiety.

From the Jungian perspective of ego psychology, with the second question Homer asks what was the archetypal, eternal ("the gods that are forever") presence behind the human behavior and events.

Perhaps the difference in critical attention to the poet's questions reflects the difference in the affective linking that, in the current spirit of the time, is present between the human theme—still very recognizable within our psyche—and the divine dimension of those ancient times, for which the link has been erased, in the West, by ages of inactivity and cognitive disconnectedness.[28]

The aggressive, territorial, competitive, and sexually exploitative instincts of the male archetype captured in the first theme are still deeply imbedded in the modern psyche of primarily patriarchal societies, albeit under cover from more or less thin layers of civilization and, occasionally, of culture. The western reader of either gender has the instinctual capacity to relate, or even identify, with the Greek thrust about power, about women as possessions, symbols of sexual potency and objects of trade, and with the fierce confrontations to establish the "alfa male" status—the hero status. Close reproductions of the symbolism contained in the violent rivalry between Achilles and Agamemnon continue to surround us today with worrisome frequency. We share through the millennia these dark components of the spirit of the depth, these archetypal derivatives from the primal evolutionary drives of territoriality and dominance.

It is much more difficult for the modern reader to experiment how the divine element was perceived by the humans of the Bronze Age and by the audiences of the Homeric times.

The divine element, in its polytheistic configuration, suffused all aspects of life and of the physical and metaphysical worlds. The ancient written documentation that has reached us describes how Bronze Age people lived with the constant awareness of the ubiquitous presence of one deity or another who would carefully assess the level and quality of their subject's reverence and piety; they had witnessed, repeatedly, the unpredictable decisional power of the deities, a power that had to be constantly mollified and persuaded through prayers and "perfect"[29] sacrifices. In other words, they were quite aware of the constant influence from archetypal, instinctual forces upon human behavior; and of the need to contain the effects of these drives seeking fulfillment out of the collective unconscious.

We are obligated to a very significant effort in creative imagination in order to silence our agnostic stance or our monotheistic concept of an abstract, omnipresent and omniscient god, and share, even dimly, the affective experience of living in a world populated by deities.[30] "The whole cosmos throbbed with supernatural life"[31]: deep in sea caves or in the forge of a volcano; in springs, and rivers, rocks and trees, and hunting in the woods, where unaware passers-by would pay with their life for the intrusion in the deity's privacy. "These were not mere abstractions, but vital living entities. Even substances like silver and fire were regarded conscious living forces endowed with human emotions."[32] This ever-present and all-infusing numinosity finds its psychological equivalent in the realm of the archetypes: the universal system of organizing themes that may cascade to the human level and populate it in specific and complex ways, often obscure and conflicting, largely indifferent to the effects on the human subject.

This is the affective dimension of the relationship between the gods and the Bronze Age, and even Classical Greece, humans; it was a relationship that Homer deeply felt as immanent and pervasive, and that he richly described over and over, in its multiple and varied manifestations, throughout the entire epic.[33] It is a relationship that one needs to experience at some affective level in order to absorb the essentiality of the theme of piety—and impiety—that Homer introduces with line 7 of Book I.[34] Impiety is indeed the fundamental trigger for the strife. However, after Calchas reveals the impiety, the issue quickly fades in importance during the following discussions among the Greeks. No immediate prayers are raised, nor are expressions of sorrow, even from Nestor, the most enlightened and allegedly pious among the Greeks. For over 200 lines (l. 100-307) the attention is focused exclusively on the strife. As I described, Agamemnon reluctantly agrees to send back Chryses' daughter—and he will make sure to send with her appropriate sacrifice—but he demands immediate equivalent compensation. After heated exchanges with Achilles, who clearly does his best to create the rift, Agamemnon decides to requisition Achilles' prize woman, Briseis.

The argument between the two mortals, when analyzed against this background, is worth a detailed studying. The entire dispute becomes focused on the theme of women as excellent prizes, sexual objects, properties of men. The army is appeased when promised "deep bosomed"[35] Trojan women to warm their beds.[36] Achilles swears that the entire Greek army and Agamemnon will pay dearly for the affront to his honor, and seeks the help of his divine mother. That seems to be the dynamic element moving the two protagonists of the strife: not the concern about having acted in an impious way toward Apollo but rather a competitive challenge about the (sexual[37]) ownership of a woman: a reenactment of the eternal Oedipal struggle.

BOOK I: PSYCHODYNAMIC ANALYSIS OF THE STRIFE AND ITS MAIN CHARACTERS

The figure of Agamemnon is depicted in noticeably negative terms; we are immediately presented with his demeaning treatment of the priest of Apollo, with his reluctance to expiate for the act on impiety, and with his offense to the honor of Achilles by stripping him of his prize-woman; additionally, his decision to demand a retribution of equal value from the army or from the other kings seems to be—and possibly is—unfair. Indeed, wounded honor and failed, corrupt leadership are the central elements to Dr. Shay's masterpiece on war trauma and the undoing of character among Vietnam veterans, as well as in the reconstruction by Dr. Alexander of her hero figure.

Contrary to Agamemnon, Achilles appears to be the character who stands up against unfairness and an inept commander-in-chief with his failed leadership; by calling the people to assembly he seems to show great pity for the Achaeans; with this act he "declares himself the hero of the Achaean army and the hero of the epic."[38]

An assessment of the exchanges between Achilles and Agamemnon reveals a more complex picture. The strife is predetermined and unavoidable, in order to activate the entire set of events that will culminate with the death of Hector and the fall of Troy. The sequence of statements, though, as Homer builds up the confrontation, is principally focused on the description of the characters rather than on the event itself,[39] and what Homer has them say to each other provides an insight on how he feels about them and about the conflictual issues that they play out.

After having been accused of impiety, Agamemnon, as reported, becomes enraged and invests the seer Calchas with harsh, rage-filled words: "Prophet of evil, *never* yet have you given me a favorable prophecy; *always* it is dear to your heart to prophesy evil" (emphasis mine). Homer is silent about any past evil prophecy that Agamemnon seems to refer to, but his silence is very loud. The theme of past acts of impiety had to be in his mind, for him to have Agamemnon express it, and most likely he was thinking to the recent horrendous parricide at Aulis. Other rhapsodes, like Stasinus of Cyprus, a semi-legendary early Greek poet considered the author of the Cypria,[40] and the tragic poets Aeschylus and Euripides, describe that event, which sheds light on the furious statement of Agamemnon (and on the otherwise poorly explainable highly confrontational behavior of Achilles). According to these sources, when the Greek expedition was collected in Aulis and ready to sail for Troy, Agamemnon shot a stag and enraged the goddess Artemis (sister, by the way, of Apollo!) who "sent stormy winds and, prevented them from sailing."[41] When the inclement, blustery weather continued without any sign of lightning, the Greek army became increasingly restless and threatened to leave the expedition and return home. Odysseus asked Calchas to reveal the cause of the off-season unrelenting storm and the seer explained that Artemis had been offended by Agamemnon's boasting remarks, and only by sacrificing his daughter Iphigenia on the goddess' altar could the king of Argos appease her.[42] Agamemnon tricked his wife Clytemnestra into bringing the daughter to Aulis from Argos, with a promise to marry her to Achilles[43] — who became aware of the trick and felt gravely abused, deceived, and dishonored![44] — and then cut Iphigenia's throat on the goddess' altar (here the story offers diverse endings, in that some say that the goddess saved Iphigenia at the last moment and brought her to run her temple in Tauris). The psychodynamics of the confrontation in the *Iliad* become much clearer against this background; they are the reenactment of an old and grave conflict with striking similarities to the present one.[45] Homer did not mention the dreadful parricide — that will ultimately cause Agamemnon's death by the hands of a revenge-ridden Clytemnestra — but he knew that the tragedy at Aulis was familiar to his audiences and he wanted them to remember it. The collective shadow of that shameful episode upon the characters of its protagonists and of the entire Achaean army was a serious one, though deeply buried under the glitter of the ultimate victory and the exploits of the Greek heroes. Homer's silent judgment about the parricidal father, about the other kings and the entire army that asked for and allowed the sacrifice, and Achilles who did nothing to stop it, transpires in the present reenactment, nevertheless.[46] We are left to reflect why Homer does not let Agamemnon mention Aulis directly, but only in such oblique way. Some concern restrained Homer on this topic. The process of therapy has demonstrated that what is not told but hinted at in oblique, cryptic ways, is generally a most informative indication of the complexes and of the defensive activation in the analysand's mind. Freud educated us on projection, when we use others — real or imagined — to express what we cannot reveal about ourselves. The theme was on Homer's mind and had to be told: he wanted to remind audiences that the impiety and the disregard for fairness and ethics were a long-standing pattern for Agamemnon and the Greek army, rather than a singular episode prone to be condoned. However, a rhapsode from late Bronze Age or archaic colonized Ionia could not do what Aeschylus — an Athenian whose tragedies had repeatedly captured the first prize in public contexts — did several centuries later, without putting his work and his life in great jeopardy. Similarly, Homer would be at risk to openly remind his audiences that Achilles had already professed at Aulis a deep commitment to a woman (he promised a betrothal) but then backed out, unwilling to fight the same stronger adversary. His honor had been more gravely injured at Aulis than now; yet he did not confront Agamemnon and sailed with the rest of the army.[47]

At this point, with a deeper understanding concerning the probable dynamics at the root of the conflict, in the Greek camp and in the mind of Homer as well, we may return to the analysis of its evolution.

Agamemnon proceeds by agreeing to return Chryseis to her father. He demands, though, adequate remuneration, given that he is doing it for the good of them all. Achilles is the first — and only one — to respond. The silence of all the other kings is illuminating. It is not out of fear that they do not object to Agamemnon: they are all kings, and leaders of strong contingents; neither Diomedes not Odysseus nor the two Aias will hesitate to rebuff Agamemnon quite strongly in more than one occasion. Therefore, Homer may imply through their silence that all the other parties consider Agamemnon's request of a compensation as understandable and ultimately not debatable, even if unfair for the recipient (gods are traditionally unfair as well). The impiety was a collective act, in that there was neither awareness nor opposition to it[48]; and the release of Chryseis, the priest's daughter, is for the good of the entire army; it is inappropriate then, seems to declare Agamemnon, that he should be the only one to pay for it.[49]

Achilles' way of confronting Agamemnon escalates rapidly. The young man, fully confident in his physical superiority and in his predominance as a warrior, furiously challenges the older, covetous Commander, whose demands the youngster considers unacceptable. What we have a glimpse at, what Homer captures, is the eternal archetypal theme of a rebellious, omnipotent-feeling youth (and new order), confronting the representation of a largely negative parental archetypal image for the ownership of a contended feminine and for the alpha status. Achilles is looking for blood, for the Oedipal symbolic patricide. Only the intervention of Athene (the feminine wise warrior numen) avoids immediate tragedy.

By contrast, Agamemnon restrains his words; he is, after all, very skilled in diplomacy and political compromises; only when left with no other choice he responds in tone and describes Achilles as "most hateful to me are you of the kings, nurtured by Zeus, for always is strife dear to you, and wars and battle"[50] (not by chance alone these will be the same words that Homer will have an angry Zeus speak to Ares[51] in Book V).

My understanding of the strife scene differs somewhat from that of Dr. Shay (and Alexander), and that explains the subsequent difference in the interpretation of the wounded honor and failed leadership issues. In Dr. Shay's reading the content is present, but the context is different. When he compares the core factors activating the Vietnam syndrome to the dynamics playing out in the Greek camp I cannot avoid the impression that the events and words presented and spoken during the altercation are viewed through the lenses of modern revisionism: cognitively very coherent with our modern experiences — and therefore beautifully adapting to the deeply felt and understood experiences of the Vietnam warriors — as long as they are referred to, and interpreted through, our current spirit of the time: affectively disconnected from the collective spirit of Homer's sociocultural niche. Two considerations left me perplexed about the true causal similarity, beyond the superficially apparent one, between the two situations. I have already discussed the one concerning the domain of the divine; now I will address the domain of the human.

Dr. Shay describes Agamemnon's behavior as deeply unfair and "a betrayal of the moral order of the soldier by a commander" in that he wrongfully seized the prize of honor from Achilles (p. 3). He then continues: "A modern equivalent might be a commander telling a soldier: 'I'll take that Congressional Medal of Honor of yours, because I don't have one.'"

The strife scene, however, presents a more complex set of conditions. Agamemnon—a truly unpleasant character and seedy Commander-in-Chief[52]—is obliged to give up his Congressional Medal of Honor in order to save the army: an army that had no comment to make when their Commander refused to accept the ransom offered by the father-priest: it was his right to keep his prize of honor. No one at that moment raised any alarm to any possible cloud of impiety as the one that would soon start brooding over the horizon, nor saw it later on, to explain the divine plague. Everyone, even Achilles, needed a Calchas to connect the dots. Homer makes abundantly clear that Agamemnon does not bend to give up his medal out of a sudden surge of religious guilt, but under the sense of his responsibility toward the wellbeing of the army (a step that Achilles was not willing to take). The sacrifice of his Medal was not any easier than the one requested from Achilles. The difference was, as Nestor points out, that Agamemnon did not receive the baton from a majority vote of the other kings or from a structured (political) system as the American military and its president and Commander-in-Chief, but from Zeus. This difference between Agamemnon and the other sceptered kings is pointed out repeatedly throughout the epic![53]

The theme of honor will be discussed again; presently, though, it appears that in Homer's mind its relationship to the present affront is not as clear-cut as many scholars want to depict it. Even the goddesses consider the lost prize "redeemable" with three times its value in other gifts; certainly not worth the destruction of an entire army. Homer actually has the two goddesses tell Achilles to stop the strife; he seems in this way to reinforce the implication that the wrath of Achilles is a well-entrenched rage that makes him disdain even the demands of the gods. The present injury to his honor sounds like a justification at best.

Briseis per se, as a person and not as representative of a honor-prize, is practically not existent. There is no statement of love; his tears when she is taken away may be primarily for the completed affront against "the best of the Achaeans." To his mother he describes her as his prize taken away by Agamemnon; and Thetis uses the same words to repeat that description to Zeus.

What seems to remain, as basis for the strife, is perhaps deep-seated envy for the title of Commander-in-Chief,[54] mixed with deep-seated rage, and blood lust, from the still open grave wounds that as an adolescent he suffered at Aulis. Agamemnon, the severe father-master, robbed his younger rival/son of his woman twice. The ultimate reparation is death/parricide. We heard Agamemnon point to the choleric character of Achilles, with his statement "for always is strife dear to you." Homer describes repeatedly the compulsion of Achilles to drown his own psychic distress in the blood of others. Already in book I he asks for Zeus to help the Trojans "pen in those others, the Achaeans, among the stern of their ships and around the sea as they are killed, so that they may have profit of their king."

An ulterior significant component to the analysis of the strife is represented by the figure of Nestor as personification of Greek wisdom and its role in moderating and defusing conflict. This role, openly affirmed from the beginning of the epic, becomes obfuscated by several contradictions during Homer's progressive development of the character. Nestor's advices are usually preceded by long-winded boastful recollections of his own great, heroic deeds in similar circumstances. They can be practically ineffectual, as are his interventions in Book I and his advice in Book IX to send an embassy to Achilles (one would expect him to lead it, but he sends others instead). They can be quite wrong, as was his acceptance of Agamemnon's disastrous dream in Book II (a "destructive Dream" that in Homer imagination had used Nestor's likeness as the carrier of the deceit![55]), or his suggestion to build a wall without requiring the proper reverence to the gods[56]; its consequences were furious complaints by Apollo and Poseidon to Zeus, and a great flood [57] that Prof. Morris links to the Near Eastern great flood tradition mentioned in the twelve cuneiform tablets from Nineveh on the Epic of Gilgamesh and his close friend Enkidu.[58] Or the advice can prove to be dangerous and even deadly, as the one to Patroclus in Book XI.[59]

The reason that stirred Homer to consistently depict the magniloquent, paternalistic but rather ineffective aspect of the Gerenian knight is obscure; perhaps it represented an unspoken critical evaluation of how the Greek-Nestorian values of justice actually proved to be when applied to colonized Ionia. What emerges is an overall questionable view of the effectiveness of Greek wisdom and reason when presented with an escalation of the aggressive drive, when confronted by Greek hubris, and when challenged by tense, confrontational relationships.[60]

BOOK IX: THE STRIFE AND THE WRATH, CONTINUED

Homer revisits and reaffirms in further details the dynamics of the strife in Book IX, after time has elapsed since its explosive beginning. The poet describes the arrival to the hut of Achilles of three of his best friends,[61] Odysseus, Aias, and Phoenix,[62] who have come to present the peace offerings of Agamemnon and to plead for the entire Achaean army. The exchanges among the characters, as Homer articulates them, highlight once more the obstinate stance of Achilles. Three times the poet presents, through the words and pleas of the visitors, all the variables that Achilles should weight against the anger; three times the audience is faced with a variety of defensive rationalizations that in Pelides' mind justify the persistence and inflexibility of his position.

Odysseus is the first to speak and express his concerns. He cautions Achilles: "On yourself will sorrow come hereafter, nor can healing be found for a harm once done."[63] He describes how honor would be restored to him beyond measure by the public apology from Agamemnon and the list of offerings to accompany the return of "intact" Briseis. Homer certainly gave a lot of attention to that stunning list.[64] It is difficult to understand why Homer went so overboard with it; perhaps he wanted to prove how valuable was the return of Achilles, at this point of the losing battle, for Agamemnon and for the army as well; or he wanted to reinforce the fact that no amount of "honor" would satisfy Achilles, and therefore honor was not the main determinant of the strife,[65] but rather its justification.

He then adds that Achilles, even if he cannot stop hating the Atreides, should at least have pity for the rest of the Achaeans, who would honor him as a god; he could also have a better chance at killing Hector, who is now coming near the huts of the Myrmidons while fighting inside the Greek camp.

Achilles answers to Odysseus that neither Agamemnon nor the Danaans will be able to persuade him "since it is clear there was to be no thanks for warring against the foe without respite,"[66] nor for "fighting with warriors for their women's sake"[67]; and he boasts about the twenty-three cities that he has conquered. He adds that Agamemnon "has taken and keeps my wife, the darling of my heart. Let him lie by her side and take his joy"[68]; Achilles implies that he would not take her back even if she were indeed "inviolate" by Agamemnon. He confirms that he will in the morrow launch his ships and return to Phthia, his homeland; he repeats that Agamemnon "utterly he has deceived and wronged me. Never again will he deceive me with words; this is enough for him."[69] (This being deceived by words sounds like another reference to Aulis; in the present situation he was certainly wronged, but not deceived; the old deception of the false promise used by Agamemnon in Aulis seems to percolate through and add its emotional load to the present confrontation.) Of the two fates that his mother described to him—to die young at Troy and acquire a "glorious renown," or to return to Phthia to a long-married life—he has decided to choose the second. Once more, Achilles concludes informing the Achaeans that he will not be available to save them, "because of the fierceness of my anger."[70]

Then is the turn of old Phoenix, his mentor and caregiver since childhood, who reminds Achilles how he reared him with deep love. "For with no other would you go to the feast or take meat in the hall, till I had set you on my knees."[71] He pleads Pelides to "master your proud spirit; nor must you have a pitiless heart. Even the very gods can bend, though theirs is even greater excellence and honor and might."[72] He reminds Achilles how Agamemnon is offering public apologies and how has carefully chosen the dearest friends of Pelides as heralds, and cautions him that "it would be a harder task to save the ships when they are already burning."[73] The Achaeans would honor him as a god if he came to their rescue.

Phoenix also recalls that: "With you the old horseman Peleus sent me on the day when he sent you out from Phthia to Agamemnon, a mere child, knowing nothing as yet of evil war, not of assemblies in which men become preeminent." All translations that I consulted do not say how old young Achilles was at that time, but the Greek text describes him as a "πέμπε νήπιον," "a five-year-old child."[74] The Epic Cycle tells us that Achilles was possibly fifteen, during the first failed Achaean expedition against Troy. This much earlier visit to the court of Agamemnon was probably in character with the habit of sending a young future heir to the court of a powerful king for rearing, training, and diplomacy; Phoenix tells how Peleus had put him in charge of his son's education: "For this reason he sent me to instruct you in all these things."

It must have been a rather prolonged stay, and it is hard to imagine why such a sustained association between them would never come up, either during their wrathful altercation or later on as an attempt to heal the schism, unless something highly troublesome had happened between them, to load the experience with a significant negative affect. Agamemnon, who—a child himself—had had to witness his adulterous mother killed by his father, may not have been very inclined toward another very precocious and temperamental child who had an immortal mother; given his suspicious and angry character he may have been a very difficult paternal substitute. Achilles may have had great difficulty in not receiving anymore the attention he had gotten at the court of his father, and may have been incensed by Agamemnon's display of a power, and a kingdom, far superior to the one of Peleus in Phthia. Doted as he was with a choleric temperament highly sensitive to offense and debasement, real or imagined (as he will amply confirm in his middle-late twenties), the child had probably already found quite difficult to deal with an imperious and critical Agamemnon. One is left to speculate why Homer felt it necessary to mention this remote event, and to do so at this time, during the momentous embassy that recapitulates the intense, destructive, and in a way highly mystifying strife between the two of them.

Achilles is rather dismissive of his old mentor's pleas. Those tender memories from his infancy raise no echo in his heart. He criticizes Phoenix for not being exclusively on his side and discounts the army's gratitude: "in no way have I need of this honor; honored I have been, I think, by the dispensation of Zeus, which will be mine among the beaked ships."[75] He then directs Patroclus to prepare a bed for Phoenix, so that the old man could sail home with the Myrmidons in the morning.

Then Aias Telamon tells Odysseus that they should leave. They have failed their mission, because "Achilles has worked up to fury the proud heart within him, hard man, nor does he regard the love of his comrades with which we honored him among the ships above all others . . . pitiless one!"[76] Speaking in the spirit of his time he reminds Achilles that "a man accepts recompense even from the slayer of his brother, or for his dead son. . . . But as for you, the gods have put in your breast a heart that is obdurate and evil because of one girl only; but now we offer you seven, far the best that there are, and many other gifts beside…"[77]

For Achilles, though, friendships and the special love he received from his comrades during the past nine long years are not sufficient to appease his rage. Once more he returns to the theme of his rage at Agamemnon who "worked an indignity on me among the Argives."[78] He will think of war only if Hector attacks the huts and ships of the Myrmidons "as he slays the Argives and has burned the ships with fire. But around my hut and my black ship I think Hector will be stayed, eager though he is for battle."[79]

It is difficult to read these renewed characterological representations of Achilles and not question whether Homer did indeed write the *Iliad* to glorify Pelides. By the time he answers the heralds, in Book IX, Achilles could not have avoided having seen the Trojans and allies break through the wall, force the Achaeans to retreat, and fight them among the ships. The action is very close to the encampment of the Myrmidons and the dire aspect of the situation could not be missed. Homer describes in vivid terms the din of battle, the clanging of bronze, the screams, the roars of Poseidon the like of ten thousand warriors. He could have formulated the entire episode differently, to convey the great importance, for Agamemnon and for the entire army, of Achilles returning to the war, while sheltering Pelides from the obstinate repetitions of his unrelenting rage. The poet could have hinted at some softening in Achilles' mind, at the potential for reconsideration of his wrath against the Army, should the situation of the Achaeans worsen even more; and then he could have proceeded—as he did—to create some sort of emergency—like a contingent of Trojans attacking the Myrmidons' camp—that could have stirred the concern of Achilles and engaged Patroclus and his Myrmidons to reenter the fray. Instead, the encounter that Homer describes is not very edifying to the character of Achilles; the embassy shows primarily the profound apology of Agamemnon, his resolve to sacrifice his own honor in order to pacify the son of Peleus, and the pleadings of great warriors, peers of Achilles, who do not mind bending their own pride by asking him for leniency, in the name of all the Achaeans.

Homer provides glimpses of an Achilles who could be generous in certain situations, gifted with gentle aspects, as his skill with the lyre and his relationship with Patroclus. He shows great understanding for the tragedy of Achilles' fate, which he describes repeatedly in touching images filled with empathy. Nevertheless, he is also very graphic and insistent in painting a generally negative profile of Pelides: from the overall figure of the "warrior archetype" with his grandiose, god-like self-image to the absence of boundaries to his anger, and to his disregard for human and divine values. And he puts in sharp relevance the deeply dark side of Achilles' psyche: his grandiose sense of self (he repeatedly describes himself as the greatest warrior of all), his lust for battle and gory conquests, and his extreme vulnerability to any real or perceived offense. He may be physically invulnerable, but he is emotionally defenseless. When psychically wounded, he turns to the defensive system he knows the best: fighting and killing; punishing the sources of the injury by violent death and the spilling of blood; burying the pain from the psychic wound under all-consuming anger and destructive rage.

HOMER'S STANDING ON THE CAUSALITY OF GREEK WRATH: CONCLUSIVE REMARKS

Having closely looked at repeated behaviors and statements, at what was said and what was not said or could be avoided or said differently, we have collected sufficient material for an analysis of the attitude of Homer toward the events surrounding the rage of Achilles, and for the psychodynamic understanding and exploration of his mental organization and of his affective links to the main characters..

Three variables have been postulated at the root of the strife with Agamemnon: challenge for the top leadership, grief from a lost love, and honor.

What Homer seems to overtly express through his characters is that the context about chief leadership should not be an issue. While not only Achilles, but also several of the other kings have harsh words about the fighting spirit of Agamemnon and his intermittent cowardice,[80] there is never a real challenge to his role as chief commander. Several Scholiasts in times to come would attribute his highest status among the other kings to the fact that he commanded a greater number of soldiers than anyone else; in reality we heard that his mandate comes directly from Zeus and therefore, in the spirit of his time, it is beyond discussion. Everyone is free to leave the alliance of the kings, unless bound by the old promise that Tyndareus requested from the contenders to the hand of Helen

(Achilles was too young to be there). But whoever remains in the alliance, unconditionally accepts Agamemnon as the commander-in-chief.

Homer, though, inserts some wordings and statements that suggest how Achilles may consider himself as the one most entitled to that position; he repeatedly describes how he is "the best of the Achaeans," flaunts his many warring feats, and the psychodynamic theme of his feeling unfairly relegated to a subordinate role may be traced back to the first expedition when, still an adolescent—so the lore of the time told—he saved the day for the Achaeans by severely wounding king Telephus.[81] Already in the initial heat of the strife some of the long-standing resentment between the two characters seeps out; Achilles questions Agamemnon "how can any Achaean eagerly obey your words?"[82]; Agamemnon, in justifying to Nestor his wrath, complains, "This man is minded to be above all others, over all he is minded to hold sway and be king among all, and to all give orders; of which there is one, I think, who will not obey him."[83] Agamemnon seems to bring to the surface a recognizable pattern of behavior from Achilles, characterized by resistance to accept a subordinate or even equal role, not only from Agamemnon but from the other leaders as well. This behavior is clearly manifest in Book IX, in the way Achilles relates to Odysseus and Aias, and—by inference—to all the other kings. However, to openly challenge the leadership would be an act of grave disobedience toward the Godhead; therefore his resentment needs to seek some other sort of expression, as the annihilation of Agamemnon by some other means ("the full price of all the outrage" to which he alludes in Book IX).

By the end of the epic Briseis—ostensibly the primary cause of the strife, either as Achilles' beloved or as a prize symbol, or both—has appeared three times: briefly, a figure without definition, in Book I, when she is taken away by Agamemnon's heralds; she reappears, vibrantly alive in her emotions and words, in Book XIX, when she cries over Patroclus; and she lays in bed beside Achilles in Book XXIV: the last glimpse that the *Iliad* offers of her and of her master-lover.

It would make little clinical sense to rely on the sociocultural value system of our time in order to interpret the affective valence of the relationship between these two characters,[84] and its significance, as it transpires in the writings of Homer almost three thousand years ago. The pattern of openly expressed, affectionate, intimate exchanges is subject to multiple variables that change with each particular sociocultural milieu. To mention but a few, the status and role of women in a specific social system, and the social judgment of male overt expression of emotions, can play primary roles in the quality and content of heterosexual exchanges.

However, the poet was quite accomplished with words and with the portrayal of characters: we may search for comparable settings to analyze the words he used and those he chose not to use, as well as non-verbal shows of affective activation, and how such choices influenced the emotional resonance of the characters involved. He had no hesitation to express caring words elsewhere, as, repeatedly, between Hector and Andromache, as we will discuss later on[85]; he could very perceptively bring to the surface emotions, whenever he shared them and felt them fitting the characters.

In the case of Briseis, it does not appear, from the wordings used by Homer, that in his mind she represented a true love object for Achilles. Not once does Homer have Achilles speak to her directly, even one single word: not when in Book I she comes out of his hut, accompanied by Patroclus, to be taken to Agamemnon by the heralds[86]; nor when in Book XIX she is returned to Achilles, who does not even look at her: while she cries on the body of Patroclus he talks to the elders. Certainly not in his bed, during his last appearance. Despite some protestations of emotional significance she is at best a lust object, a coveted sexual prize. Indeed, he calls her repeatedly a prize; her importance apparently comes from the fact that she was not part of a standard distribution of bounty among the troops, but a unique prize given to him by the Achaeans[87] — and, apparently, by Agamemnon himself[88] — as a sign of special recognition for his martial feats.

For an understanding of Achilles' real love for a person, and grief for a loss, Homer offers the comparison of his reactions to the loss of Patroclus and to the loss of Briseis; Achilles sleeps with captured fair-cheeked Diomede a few days after Briseis was taken away, just following his impassioned speech to Odysseus and Aias about having lost "his beloved" to Agamemnon; while even his own mother fails to convince him to sleep with someone, in order to find some solace from the wrenching loss of Patroclus.

I have explored the theme of the injured honor (τιμή) at the emergence of the strife and in the exchanges between Achilles and the ambassadors in Book IX. The thrust of my analysis is not the same as that of the very exhaustive scholarly studies that were overall focused on building the case for the severity of the affront performed by Agamemnon. Rather, my analysis addresses Homer's personal opinion about the character of Achilles, and the poet's emotional link to the transferred rage.

Most of the studies I became aware of describe how in the *Iliad* the terms time' and menis are used exclusively in reference to the strife and to Achilles; Homer turned to the special, out of the ordinary, meaning of these words to convey the exalted and tragic dimensions of Pelides, with his semi-divine status. Concurrently, Homer hints over and over, using very similar statements by many characters, to the insufficient correlation between the injury and the response, even if the old conflict at Aulis is added to the scale. Actually, in one of his mirroring scenes, Homer in Book XXIII describes — in a humorous but still significant way — how Pelides acted as Agamemnon had done when he decided to take back the prize that Antilochus, the son of Nestor, had won by arriving second in the chariots race,[89] in order to give it to Eumelus, who had arrived last with a broken chariot. The statement of Antilochus "Achilles, I shall be very angry with you . . . for you are about to rob me of my prize"[90] is an admirable counterpoint to what Achilles blamed Agamemnon for in Book I: "you even threaten that you will yourself take away from me the prize for which I toiled much."[91]

No one questions that the honor of Achilles was wounded, when a very beautiful sexual prize was taken away from him (partly out of his own doing), but the offered recompense was so extravagantly superior to the offense, as Aias points out, that anyone else would have relented. Instead Achilles answers that ". . . not even so will Agamemnon any more persuade my heart <u>until he has paid the full price</u> of all the outrage that stings my heart" (emphasis mine).[92] One is left to wonder what would the full price be, given that Agamemnon has voluntarily fully stripped himself in public of his honor and is openly pleading for the forgiveness of Achilles. Perhaps Pelides expected that the army, and the other kings, would strip Agamemnon of his command and would pass the scepter of Zeus to him. Homer actually gives him that, not by words but by facts; as we will see in his aristeia, Achilles is the only hero figure on the battlefield, to lead the Achaean army in slaughtering the Trojans and Hector.

Without having to say it explicitly, Homer built a powerful demonstration of the fact that nothing except major bloodshed and innumerable sufferings and deaths could placate a spiteful and "pitiless" Achilles: the psychodynamic analysis of this narrative points to a constellated search for a primal oedipal triumph and a vindication from a history of narcissistic wounds since infancy and childhood.

The total subjugation of his psyche to the blinding and all-possessing power of the wrath confirms that his complex has become triggered, or, in the Jungian term, constellated, by the archetypal jealousy and wrath motifs of Hera and Athene, the everlasting consequence of their loss of honor and feminine primacy to the rival Aphrodite. Achilles has become a tool and vehicle for their revenge.

NOTES

1. Similarly, the closing lines of a book, or of an analysis, signify and encapsulate the completion of the project, its ultimate finality, when all that there was to tell has been told.

2. Μῆνιν ἄειδε, θεά, Πηληϊάδεω ' Ἀχιλῆος οὐλομένην (*Iliad*, Book I, l. 1-2)

3. Τίς τ' ἄρ σφωε θεῶν ἔριδι ξυνέηκε μαχεσθαι; Ibid., l. 8.

4. As with other Greek heroes, Agamemnon, appointed by Zeus as Commander in Chief, does not appear very concerned about antagonizing some deity. Diomedes will chase Ares and wound him, as well as Aphrodite (*Iliad* Book V, ll. 334 ff., 855 ff.); Achilles will challenge the god Scamander, who will be of a different make than Ares,

and Pelides will risk to end up drowning without Hera telling Hephaestus to fight Scamander, fire fighting water. Agamemnon is clearly more concerned about his honor, should he be forced to give away his prize. The danger of impiety does not seem to cross his mind, nor is it apparently a concern to any of the other kings, or to the army.

5. "... to Chryses his priest the son of Atreus had done dishonor" (*Iliad*, Book I, l. 11).
6. Ibid., l. 106.
7. Ibid., ll. 116 ff.
8. Ibid., l. 122.
9. Ibid., ll. 128-129.
10. "Since you ask me to give her back." Ibid., 134.
11. Ibid., ll. 149 ff.
12. Ibid., ll.172-177.
13. Ibid., ll. 185-187.
14. Ibid., ll. 208 ff.
15. "You heavy with wine, with the face of a dog but the heart of a deer..." Ibid., ll. 225–233.
16. Ibid., l. 299.
17. *Iliad*, Book I, ll. 409 ff.
18. *Iliad*, Book I, ll. 488 ff.
19. *Iliad*, Book VIII, ll. 80 ff.
20. *Iliad*, Book II, ll. 370 ff.
21. In the *Odyssey*, Telemachus encounters him seven or eight years after the fall of Troy, still very active and ageless, able still to drink to his heart's content, and still as wordy as ever! The last one to retire to bed, "beside him the lady his wife brought him loving embrace and comfort." (*Odyssey*, Book III l. 403).
22. To quote a few more recent ones: Eduard Schwyzer (1931); Carl Darling Buck (1949); Calvert Watkins (1977); Patrick Considine (1985); Leonard Mueller (1996).
23. As a telling and tragic outcome of their dynamics it will be Patroclus, the closest and most respectful of his comrades, who will disobey his Commander-in-Chief in a far-reaching way.
24. "... but in the tenth (day) Achilles called the army to the place of assembly; for the goddess, white-armed Hera, had put it in his heart; for <u>she</u> pitied the Danaans because she saw them dying." *Iliad*, Book I, ll. 54-55 (emphasis mine).
25. This feminine image will keep returning, through the various goddesses, his mother Thetis and mostly his other-self Patroclus.
26. *Argonautica*, Book 4, ll. 799 ff.
27. Ibid. ll. 866 ff.
28. Or, always in Jungian terms, the difference between the spirit of the time, the current events, and the spirit of the depth, the archetypal templates.
29. "... we offered to the eternals perfect hecatombs..." *Iliad*, Book 2, l. 306; "Did Hector then never burn for you thighs of bulls and goats without blemish?" (Apollo reminding the gods) *Iliad*, Book 24, ll. 33-34.
30. In the West the polytheistic theology lost its numinosity by becoming a set of mythical stories, a fable, profoundly separated from the "true monotheistic religions" that followed it, with the possible exclusion of the Catholic faith that has maintained a significant Goddess figure and has recreated a very rich pantheon of minor gods, the Saints.
31. T. Bryce: *Life and Society in the Hittite World*, p. 135.
32. T. Bryce; Ibid.
33. The polytheistic systems were in a way metaphorical representation of the complex archetypal domain, while monotheism may be seen as an attempt to suppress its diversity and its shadow aspects, in favor of an all-white psychic order.
34. The interpretation of the ancient experience of the divine based on our present standing—in the ongoing transformation of its metaphorical meaning—raises the question of a significant revisionism of that divine dimension that infused all aspects

of Bronze Age life. Dr. Shay has an entire chapter on the Olympian gods: "Reclaiming the *Iliad*'s Gods as Metaphors of Social Power." He reports a statement by Jasper Griffin: "the gods of Homer must be faced as gods, and then we must see what we can make of them" (Shay, p. 149 ff.). This is a very interesting scholastic revisionism, excellent for a study on the evolution of the concept of the divine through the millennia, perhaps; but a psychoanalytic study of the *Iliad* requires that we, the observers, do not "make anything of them" (which would be a countertransferential contamination) but try, in a certain way, to have them make something of us, to experience them as Homer and the prehomeric warriors did: to shift into a condition of intersubjectivity with the analysand.

35. ". . . will deep-bosomed (literally βαθύκολπος: firm-breasted) Trojan and Dardanian women make lament night and day . . ." (*Iliad*, Book XVIII, l. 339).

36. "Let no man make haste to depart homewards until each has lain with the wife of some Trojan" (*Iliad*, Book II, ll. 354-355).

37. Despite all his protestations of love ("my wife, the darling of my heart"), Achilles states that he will not want Briseis anymore, after Agamemnon has laid "by her side and take his joy" (*Iliad*, Book IX, ll. 335 ff). Note that Briseis, up to this point, is still described solely as a special prize, different than the booty from pillaging, but nothing more; as a payback for that prize Achilles demands from the gods the death of a great number of Achaeans and the burning of the ships.

38. C. Alexander, p. 18

39. "The chief greatness of the *Iliad* is in the character of the heroes . . . rather than in the actual events." Hugh G. Evelyn-White: Hesiod, p. XXXI.

40. The poem, now lost, was well known in antiquity. Herodotus refers to it (II.117). Stasinus happens to be another epic poet of the Trojan saga from Asia Minor, rather than from mainland Greece. A fragment from the Cypria (Tzetzes, Chil. XIII. 638) reports that Homer composed the Cypria and gave it to Stasinus "as a dowry with money besides"! (Hesiod, p. 497, LCL # 57).

41. From the Cypria as reported in LCL # 57 p. 493.

42. Knowledge of this previous event also explains the serious concern that Calchas has of raising Agamemnon's fury by accusing him once more of impiety!

43. The Cypria, LCL # 57, p. 495.

44. Achilles to Clytemnestra: "Your daughter shall never be slaughtered by her father since she was called mine: I shall never lend myself to your husband so that he may weave his wiles" Euripides, LCL #495, p. 271.

45. In the Cypria, Achilles quarrels with Agamemnon also in Lesbos, after the expedition left Aulis, because "he was invited late." There seems to be a long-standing rancor of some sort in Achilles toward the figure of Agamemnon and/or his role of Commander-in-Chief. And, as we will see again, Achilles was sent as a youth to the Court of Agamemnon. Could the animosity between them be rooted that far back in their relationship?

46. It took several centuries, at least to my knowledge, for the judgment to be declaimed aloud by Aeschylus. He describes how Agamemnon, with an "impious, unholy, unsanctified" mind, "hardened his heart to sacrifice his daughter that he might prosper a war waged to avenge a woman, and as an offering for the voyaging of the fleet! Her supplications, her cries of "Father," and her virgin life, <u>the commanders in their eagerness for war</u> reckoned as naught." (*Agamemnon*, ll. 223-230. In Aeschylus vol. II, LCL, 146, emphasis mine). The profound disdain of Aeschylus for the tragedy at Aulis is straightforward and unmistakable.

47. To his defense, at Aulis he probably was ten years younger; and he was not yet as seasoned as he was at Troy, after nine years of warring.

48. Achilles had asked Calchas: "Why Phoebus Apollo has conceived such anger, whether because it is of a vow that he blames us, or a hecatomb." (*Iliad*, Book I, ll. 64 ff.). Evidently no one, including Achilles, had put two and two together and had suspected Agamemnon's behavior toward the priest as impious, and connected it with the god's deadly activity.

49. "Make ready a prize at once . . . for all you see this, that my prize goes from me elsewhere." (*Iliad* Book I, ll. 118 ff.). Possibly, he perceived that his honor would suffer, should he not demand compensation by requiring that the entire army pay as well.

50. *Iliad*, Book I, ll. 175-177.

51. "Most hateful to me are you of all the gods who hold Olympus, for always strife is dear to you, and wars and fighting." *Iliad*, Book V, ll. 889 ff.

52. Politically astute, though, and ruthless. He had assured the hand of Helen to his brother Menelaus and that of Clytemnestra to himself, killing her first husband in order to clear the way; in that manner he linked holy Sparta to Mycenae and built the strongest kingdom of Bronze Age Greece—known as the Mycenean era. He was re-elected leader of the second expedition, after having led the first one to the wrong target. He successfully negotiated the crisis at Aulis, and kept the rowdy alliance together for nine years. (And he carried within himself—a child still, and his frightened younger brother hiding behind him—the image of his father throwing his naked mother to her death down a steep cliff near Tyrins, her broken body swept away by the sea waves breaking against the rocks.) All this information was available to Homer in much greater details and affective significance than to us. It was this rich narrative that contributed to the poet's complex and conflicted reconstruction of the Mycenean king's character figure.

53. "No good thing is a multitude of lords; let there be one lord, one king, to whom the son of . . . Cronos has given the scepter and judgment." *Iliad* Book II, ll. 203 ff. "the son . . . of Cronos . . . the scepter he has granted you to be honored above all" *Iliad*, Book IX, ll. 37 ff.

54. "How can any Achaean eagerly obey your words?" Achilles to Agamemnon, *Iliad* Book I ll. 150 ff.

55. Ibid, ll. 20 ff. "So he (the Dream) stood above his head, in the likeness of the son of Neleus, Nestor, whom above all the elders Agamemnon held in honor."

56. *Iliad*, Book XII, ll. 8 ff. "But against the will of immortal gods was it built."

57. Ibid., ll. 17 ff.

58. Another Achilles-Patroclus type saga originating in the Near east and most likely known to Homer since childhood.

59. *Iliad*, Book XI, ll. 796 ff.

60. A modern assessment of this figure, colored by our current sociocultural niche, could compare him to the sort of political figures common to our times, who extoll their wisdom and knowledge through tirades filled with self-aggrandizement and rhetorical expectations, but rather empty in actual delivery, or expressions of narcissistic grandeur and hunger for power!

61. Achilles receives them by saying: "Welcome, you are friends indeed that have come— the end must surely be great—you who even in my anger are to me the dearest of the Achaeans." *Iliad*, Book IX, ll. 197-198.

62. Phoenix represents a puzzle: he is a Myrmidon and as such he should not have been present at the Greek deliberations nor selected by Agamemnon to be part of the assembly. He is selected to "lead the way" to Aias and Odysseus. Homer may have chosen him in order to offer information about the childhood of Achilles and to illustrate his relationship to paternal figures. Book IX, l. 168 ff.

63. Ibid., ll. 249-250.

64. It is perhaps important to review the list in detail: "seven tripods that the fire has not touched, and ten talents of gold and twenty gleaming cauldrons, and twelve strong horses, winners in the race, that have won prizes by their fleetness. . . . And I will give seven women skilled in noble handiwork, women of Lesbos whom on the day when Achilles himself took well-built Lesbos I chose out for myself from the spoil, who in beauty surpass all the tribes of women . . . and among them will be she whom then I took away, the daughter of Briseus; and I will swear...that I never went to her bed nor slept with her . . . and if we . . . lay waste the great city of Priam, let him . . . heap up his ships with gold and bronze, and he himself choose twenty Trojan women. . . . And if we return . . . he shall be my son . . . three daughters I have . . . let him

lead as his own to the house of Peleus whichever one he will, without bride price . . . and in addition I will give him a very rich dowry. And seven well-peopled cities I will give him..." *Iliad*, Book IX, ll. 121-149. This is a very different list of gifts than the one Homer puts in the mouth of the goddesses, in Book I.

65. There is something odd about the western apotheosis of Achilles (and I was fully immersed in it). Homer's human characters—all sharing the psychosocial niche of his time—are very consistent in judging Achilles' behavior in strongly negative terms.

66. *Iliad*, Book IX, ll. 316-317.

67. Ibid., l. 327.

68. Ibid., ll.336-337.

69. Ibid., ll. 374-376.

70. Ibid., ll. 425-426.

71. Ibid., ll. 486 ff.

72. Ibid, ll. 496 ff.

73. Ibid., ll. 603 ff.

74. Ibid., ll. 438 ff. From a psychodynamic perspective this age is at the center of the Freudian Oedipal phase of development.

75. Ibid., ll. 607 ff.

76. Ibid., ll. 628 ff.

77. Ibid., ll. 632 ff (emphasis mine).

78. Ibid., ll. 647-648.

79. Ibid., ll. 652 ff.

80. His aristeia, in Book XI, is a significant one. He leads the charge of the Achaeans up to the walls of Troy, and in the process he kills eight named warriors and an uncounted but great number of Trojan foot soldiers and charioteers, from the descriptions in ll. 152 ff, and then again in ll. 177 ff. He stops after being stabbed in the arm by the eldest son of Antenor, Coon, but not before killing and beheading him.

81. Indeed, the developmental narrative of the strife assumes further clarity if it is complemented by the inclusion of the Telephus saga among its determinants. The figure of the king of Mysia (considered a son of Zeus by Hesiod), and his ordeal after Achilles wounded him when he led the Mysians and defeated the invading Achaeans, were apparently well known in antiquity and already part of the Epic Cycle. Proclus, as already mentioned, relates it as part of the Cypria; and he reports that Telephus was directed to Argos by Apollo to seek a cure for the festering wound; he allegedly forced Agamemnon, by seizing his infant son Orestes, to intercede with Achilles who eventually scraped some of the spear's rust on the wound, and it healed! In exchange, Telephus revealed the correct location of Troy. The story became the focus of plays, now lost, from all the three great Greek tragedians, and was a topic for several historians, as Apollodorus and Hyginus, among others. It is plausible that Achilles, the temperamental goddess-born adolescent, the superlative fighter, saw himself as the primary architect of the second expedition and felt quite entitled to full honors and recognition, possibly even the Zeus-sceptered leadership; after all, he had bested Agamemnon in the pivotal roles of saving the army and finding the right way!

82. *Iliad*, Book I, ll. 150 ff.

83. Ibid., ll. 287 ff.

84. It is a complex relationship. Achilles—at his best but not to her face—describes her as "my beloved wife, even If captured by my spear"; Briseis recalls how her capture implied the deaths of her husband and her three brothers by the same spear. One is left to consider whether Briseis could have felt for Achilles the same way that Achilles felt for Hector, after the killing of Patroclus, or even worse, given that her loss had been fourfold.

85. Consider also the reactions of Agamemnon when he is requested to return Chryseis. He prefers her to Clytemnestra ("she is in no way inferior to her, either in form or in stature, or in mind, or in handywork." *Iliad* Book I, ll. 114-117); note the praise to the mind and the handywork. He wants her to share his house chores, and

his bed, through old age (*Iliad*, Book I, ll. 28-31, rejected by Aristarchus). Or the exchanges between Paris and Helen in Book III. Or consider the encounter between Zeus and Hera, its culmination secreted under a golden cloud: a vivid picture of perennial archetypal images. We do not hear anything like this from Achilles.

86. Homer describes her as going with the heralds "all unwilling"; Achilles starts to cry and calls to his mother complaining that Agamemnon "has done me dishonor: for he has taken away and holds my prize, through his own arrogant act." Not his love, or his wife, or the dear to his heart; but his prize. Parenthetically, in another of Homer's many insight-provoking innuendos and distant comparisons, Achilles cries to his mother (as a child deprived of his prize?) for his own personal sorrow. Patroclus cries as a child for the sorrow of others.

87. Book I, l. 299.

88. "I will bring from here . . . all that fell to me by lot; but my prize—he who gave it to me has taken it back in his arrogant pride, lord Agamemnon, son of Atreus." Ibid., ll. 365 ff.

89. Chariots races were given great importance through the bronze and classical periods, reflecting the absolute preeminence of chariots and charioteers in Bronze Age warfare. All individuals mentioned in the *Iliad* by name, except Pandaros by his own choice, are chariot fighters. The chariot race is the first of the games that Achilles organizes immediately after Patroclus' funeral; the worth of its first and second prizes— "a woman to lead away, skilled in noble handiwork, and an eared tripod of two and twenty measures for him who should be first; and for the second . . . a mare of six years, unbroken, with a mule foal in her womb"—speaks to its foremost importance; the competitors are all high-ranking charioteers, as Eumelus, Menelaus and Diomedes; and Homer dedicates to the race almost 300 lines rich in details and in skilled, lively reports of the several events, the dangers, and the relationship between the charioteer and his animals. Such a level of descriptive attention is indicative of the importance that Homer *felt* for the race, its meaning, and its status. In comparison, the entire funeral of Patroclus (to whom the race is dedicated), from the building of the pyre to its burning, to the collection of the bones and the building of the mound, required less than 150 verses.

90. *Iliad*, Book XXIII ll. 543-544.

91. *Iliad*, Book I ll. 161-162.

92. *Iliad*, Book IX, ll. 386 ff.

FOUR
Book II: A Dynamic Analysis of the Opposing Armies

Homer, after having accompanied the squabbling gods to their respective homes and to sleep, opens Book II with the episode of the "destructive dream": a deceptive dream sent to Agamemnon by Zeus, promising that on this day the Achaeans will capture Troy. The response of Agamemnon to the dream is to call the assembly and test the army by suggesting that they follow the mandates of Zeus and sail back home. Only the intervention of Hera and Athene and Odysseus (and a few other kings) is able to stop a full rout of the entire Achaean army, eager to put the ships at sea!

Homer, in Agamemnon's words, explains the ruse solely as a test to the army. The explanation is possible, but unconvincing.[1] The soldiers, veterans of nine years spent in dire living conditions on a foreign beach, their task "wholly unaccomplished," are told by their Commander-in-Chief: "let us all obey (emphasis mine); let us flee with our ships to our dear native land; for no longer is there hope that we shall take broadwayed Troy."[2] Their eager and enthusiastic response at the order of returning to their homes is quite understandable.[3]

An alternative explanation is that Homer inserted here, under some disguise, the event of a mutiny of the Greek army in the ninth year of the war that had been part of the lore preserved in the Epic Cycle.[4] The ruse allows Homer to vividly paint the Greek soldiers' dissatisfaction with nine years of rather senseless war[5]; the episode of Thersites has a mutinous feeling and only his "court martial" by Odysseus restrains the restless Achaeans. Homer also introduces, again through the words of Agamemnon, what will be the principal theme of Book II: a description of the competing forces.[6]

After the army gets restrained by the kings and spreads in formation for battle, and after the formulaic description of Agamemnon offering the expected sacrifice, Homer starts the so-called catalogue of all the ships that sailed to Troy, with a list of the Greek forces and their captains or kings. It is indeed an immense armada: 1,122 ships in total. Homer does not tell us how large the army was, except by reporting that each ship of the Boeotians—the first contingent mentioned in the catalogue—carried "one hundred and twenty young men," and each ship of the Myrmidons carried fifty soldiers.[7] The list goes on for almost 300 lines. It is a show of Greek might, but also, as I mentioned, a source of great honor for Greek families to have the poet list their ancestors among the great heroes who sailed to fabled Troy. Homer encapsulates the unparalleled magnitude of the Greek expeditionary force in its description by the goddess Iris: "I have often before now entered into battles of warriors, but never yet have I seen an army like this in quality and size; for like leaves or sands do they come over the plain to fight against the city."[8]

Then Homer follows with the description of the Trojan and allied army, as Hector orders them to deploy in the field, and the army emerges from the ca. 0.10 mls. of the city space, where they have lived, together with the civilian population, for the past nine years. It will take sixty-five lines to list them all, starting with the Trojans and ending with the Lycians of Sarpedon. In Book VIII Homer seems to set their number at 50,000.[9] Of these, the Trojans were at the most 10,000, if one accepts the just mentioned arithmetic of Agamemnon (described in endnote 6); the rest are the famous allies, the great source of distress for the Commander-in-Chief. Their number illustrates the extent of the concern of the Near East kings to the Greek invasion, and the commitment of their response to it.

The catalog of the ships echoes similar descriptions by powerful rulers of old, boastful of the armies that they could deploy to squash their enemies. So boasted the Persian king Xerxes on his way to Greece with his immense army and fleet,[10] when he commanded that the waters of the Hellespont receive three hundred whip lashes as punishment for having storm-wrecked the pontoon bridge built by his orders across the strait.

Instead, reminders of great unevenness between opposing forces are usually brought up to highlight the superior bravery of the lesser power. In post–Homeric Greece great emphasis on the profound difference in numbers marked the exploits of Marathon, Thermopylae, and Salamis. The lament of Agamemnon about the disparity of the forces sounds more like a glorification of the Trojans, and their allies, than a glorification of the Greeks.

The psychodynamic development of highly significant, idealized, subjective realities tends to shelter them, as they emerge into consciousness and acquire constancy, from conflicting ambiguity; they are perceived, out of an almost obligatory psychic demand, as "all white" systems, protected from any of the accompanying blemishes rising out of the multidimensional confounding realm of affectivity. The pressure from conflicting representations within the complete gestalt is dealt with by activating defensive alternatives, like projecting their origin and causation upon other events (as the dream of Agamemnon or his blaming the Trojan allied forces). To the attentive listener, though, in the case of intrapsychic conflict exculpatory, protective statements only reinforce the presence of a split between the grandiose idealized image and its darker, contrasting, affect-colored version, and indicate the presence of some undercurrent of ego-dystonic affect that seeks acknowledgment and recognition. This is particularly evident when the emergence of the dark side happens already at the beginning of the story, of the analytical work, as is the case with the openings of the *Iliad*.

We are left, then, with a search for this "movement of the heart," the complex mental processes and variables that guided that young rhapsode, and transpired through the manifest product of his work. Something stimulated Homer to tarnish those visuals of Greek might with the introduction of the "mutiny" scene and with the powerful depiction of the great disparity between the opposing forces, captured in the words of Agamemnon and reinforced by the comparison between Isis' comment and the limited army that Hector could muster out of the confines of Troy, when "all the gates were opened wide, and the army rushed out, both foot soldiers and charioteers; and a great din arose."[11]

By the end of Book II Homer has spoken about one act of explicit impiety and another one implicit but strongly alluded to[12]; has explored the origins of the strife (and its unmentioned psychodynamic antecedents): has offered complex portraits of its main characters; has expounded in great details the might of the Greek army, but complicated it in the same breath with the scene of a possible mutiny and with a raucous leadership; and has pointedly and repeatedly described the disparity in manpower between the Greek army and the Trojan alliance, fully aware—as he expected his audiences to be—that despite the disparity Troy had not fallen after nine years of war, as the Greek Commander-in-Chief strongly emphasizes; and he has made sure to remind the same audiences that the presence of Achilles, during those years, has not changed the outcome, although he conquered twenty-three cities, including the rather impressive fortress of Lyrnessus, and kept Hector away from the ships and preferring to fight close to the walls.[13]

This is the visible, descriptive content that depicts already some "tension between opposites," some conflicting attitude and affective response, in Homer's mind, about the material and the roles of the characters. He did not leave behind any statement describing or expressing his own personal system of values, his likes and dislikes, his subjective definition of archetypal derivatives, and his emotional response to conflicts, relational dynamics, and the realm of the divine. In order to glimpse at his subjectivity, one needs to rely on how he expresses these personal themes through the main characters of the epic and through the affective linking—and the valence of the affects—to the two camps and cultures: the Greek and the Trojan. Words slip out, detailed components of specific situations suggest different cathectic valences than those expected by the (Greek) "spirit of the time," and they may manifest some degree of distance from the descriptive style used for the main material. All these clues provide an opening direction for the analytic work to follow.

Homer created his *Iliad* circa three millennia ago. The level of his creativity is measureless; his sense of harmony and balance, his masterly ability to deal with subtle points and counterpoints is so impressive that it is not surprising how his works survived for 3,000 years—and will continue to do so—despite the merciless effect of time upon the other works of the Epic Cycle. One must read such a master with a watchful eye on each single word he used, where, and how; on the sequence of the statements and descriptions; and on how they all participate in a precise order to give a specific definition to the entire concept. So much of his complex use of the language escaped me for years, as I read it or about it, blinded by the constraints of my spirit-of-the-time directives upon my affective response to its content and upon most scholastic renderings and interpretations.

One further consideration needs to be kept in mind. It would be an error to view the *Iliad* as a complete story of its own, and to analyze its content within the exclusive framework of those fifty-one summer days.

This approach would not fit the scope of the research. In every psychodynamic study current data must be examined and understood in the context of their extended historical development. The same applies to the *Iliad*, the emergent product of that war and the prelude to its conclusion, even if the millennia that separate us from Homer blur the relationship between his work and its historical surroundings. Should the Epic Cycle have survived in its entirety, rather than as short fragments and brief summaries written centuries after their creation, we would be in the condition to have a different sense of that entire history, the way Homer had it, imbedded in it as he was since childhood. It was probably a rich and vibrant landscape that his audiences shared as well; an entire set of sagas formed a historically integrated gestalt—sung, declaimed, narrated or whatever—of those momentous ten (or twenty, or fifty) years. Instead, we have been left with a rather deserted landscape, out of which surge, in striking contrasts of color and teeming with life, the two pinnacles of the Homeric epics.

Meagre as they are, though, the fragments and summaries of the cycle allow us to gain some insight on the extent of the data available and operative in Homer's mind.

Finally, attention needs to be given to which aspect of Homer's work is suitable, or appropriate, adaptable, to fit a psychological analysis. Many of his affectively cathected analogical images are too distant and alien; they do not allow for an intersubjective assessment of their true meaning, while these same images offer very rich material for scholarly and pleasure reading. I refer, for instance, to the animal similes that Homer uses extensively in depicting warring heroes. He mentions lions forty-five times in the *Iliad* alone, and this use has been subjected to marvelously detailed and very impressive etymological and grammatical interpretations and conclusions. What is regularly missing is the experiential intersubjective correlation with what was going on in Homer's mind as he used these similes. No person in present times, except perhaps some Masai shepherds in the Ngorongoro plain, can possibly fathom the routine encounter with lions, the only defense being a spear and a few comrades. After over two millennia of inactivation the affective reality of those encounters has faded away from the collective of modern western humans, for whom lions are limited to fiction, or to cages, or—if in the wild—they are seen from behind the shield of a vehicle or of powerful weapons that indeed "strike from afar."

In Homeric times lions had probably disappeared from the Peloponnese and the Mycenean kingdoms, but could still be found in mainland Greece and were common occurrences in Asia Minor and the Anatolian lands. As a traveler, Homer most likely encountered them more than once: the frequency and graphic intensity of his similes support the consideration that those encounters were real events, affectively present and operational in his psyche; one can experience in the description the rich presence of cathectic activity. However, for an analyst of the psyche it would be very presumptive, and guided exclusively by the spirit of our time, to pretend to share with the poet the experience of those encounters, the direction of the emotional valence and of the arousal level, their meaning, and what actually directed the choice of the words and their significance to him.[14] The analyst has therefore to limit the work to the interpretation of how the psyche of Homer related to human characters, to their interactions, and to specific events. This type of material allows for intersubjective resonance in that it carries collective archetypal derivatives that the modern reader may share.

The *Iliad*, as I mentioned earlier on, is limited to fifty-one summer days during the tenth and last year of the war. Homer had chosen this brief window to portray what was foremost significant in his mind: what he considered the pivotal closing events of a very long saga that brought dramatic and everlasting changes to the history of the entire region. The various kingdoms clearly perceived the severe threat to their independence, liberty, and culture, represented by the Greek invaders. Unmistakably, they must have realized that their best chance to repel the Achaeans was to "fight them on the beaches." Only that clear perception could have justified the extent and commitment of the allied forces, the cause of Agamemnon's bitter complaint. These allies came from close and distant lands, as far away as the Ethiopians of King Memnon,[15] some overcoming long-standing gripes with Priam, as the Amazons and their queen Penthesileia. Most of their leaders died on those Ilian fields, fulfilling the plan of Zeus. Priam spent a fortune in providing to their needs and rewarding their support; however, they did not come—and stay—solely for gold or to protect the city. The *Iliad* is their story too, more poignant than the story of a strife and the wrath of a man.

NOTES

1. "... but first I will make trial of them with words, as is customary, and tell them to flee with their benched ships..." *Iliad*, Book II, ll. 73-74. Telling the army that whoever wants should feel free to flee back home is different than telling them to follow Zeus' command and flee home!

2. Ibid., ll. 139-141.

3. Agamemnon reminds them also that: "our wives, I imagine, and little ones sit in our halls awaiting us"! Ibid., ll. 135 ff.

4. Proclus (Chrestomachy 1) mentioned it in the Cypria, and reported that Achilles had convinced the soldiers to stay; however, unless there was another mutiny in the ninth year, Achilles would have no part in the present scene: Homer tells us in Book I that Pelides did not join any more assemblies. Apollodorus (Epitomes 3.10) attributes the solution of the mutiny to Agamemnon, who turned to the Wine Growers, to whom Dionysus had granted the power of producing oil, corn, and wine from the earth, in order to relieve the supply problem of the army. This last explanation is the most plausible; it points to the dire lack of supplies, after nine years of pillage, as the reason for the mutiny. As a reminder, this is the same army that at Aulis had already threatened to leave, being tired of waiting with no rewards.

5. "... the assembly was stirred like the long waves of the Icarian sea ... they with loud shouting rushed toward the ships; and from beneath their feet the dust rose up ... and their shouting went up to heaven, so eager were they to return home ..." *Iliad*, Book II, ll. 145 ff.

6. ... for ... if the Trojans should be gathered together ... and we Achaeans should be marshaled by tens, and chose, each company of us, a man of the Trojans to pour our wine, then would many tens lack a wine pourer; so far, I say, do the sons of the Achaeans outnumber the Trojans who live in the city. But there are allies from many cities ... who ... do not allow me to sack the well-peopled city of Ilios." Ibid, II, ll.125 ff.

7. Ibid., l. 510; Book XVI l. 160. A conservative estimate shared by scholars put the number of the Greeks at Troy at over 100,000.

8. Ibid., ll. 795 ff.

9. "A thousand fires were burning in the plain and by each fire sat fifty men in the glow of the blazing fire" *Iliad*, Book VIII, ll. 562 ff. "A thousand fires" may be, however, a poetic license! It is hard to imagine 50,000 warriors fitting inside Troy!

10. Herodotus mentioned one million soldiers with an elite of ten thousand Immortals. Modern reviewers speak of a force of 60,000 men.

11. *Iliad*, Book II, ll. 809-810.

12. Any analysand who would say something like "he never showed me any support" would be asked to elaborate on that "never," a word that suggests the existence, in the subject's mind, of a negatively cathected, enduring pattern of emotional dismissal and abandonment. Homer did not elaborate on the "never" of Agamemnon because he knew that the audiences of his times would easily catch the reference, while he avoided the risk from openly mentioning it himself.

13. "So long as I was warring among the Achaeans, Hector was not minded to rouse battle far from the wall..." *Iliad*, Book IX, ll. 351 ff.

14. An example of the uncertain grounds offered by later value systems in interpreting the meaning of Homeric similes is offered by the report (Laband, p. 41) that among Zulus, still in the early 1800s, a lion was a symbol of courage, and overpowering one (literally becoming a better lion) was a mean of honoring its courage and of enhancing the image of the warrior's bravery and fighting skills, rather than a regression to bestiality.

15. The Aethiopis,1, LCL # 57, p. 507.

FIVE
Book XIX: The Transferred Wrath against the Trojans

The themes of the strife and the rage emerge once more, for their final act, in Book XIX. Achilles is still the protagonist, but the themes are transferred from Agamemnon and the Achaeans to Hector and the Trojans. Following the death of Patroclus by the hands of Hector (and the loss of his armor), the mother of Achilles, Thetis, brings to him the immortal arms forged by Hephaestus[1] and advises him to announce the end of the strife against Agamemnon at an assembly of the Achaean army. Achilles does that: Homer describes how at the assembly Pelides, speaking directly to Agamemnon, regrets that "with grief at heart we raged in soul-devouring strife for the sake of a girl"[2]; blames Briseis as the cause of it all and wishes that she had been killed by Artemis among the ships[3]; and asks Agamemnon to "rouse up speedily the long-haired Achaeans to battle, so that I may go out against the Trojans and make trial of them . . . "[4] Suddenly the loathed Achaeans are needed in the service of his new implacable hatred toward Hector and everything Trojan.

For three books (less the brief "battle of the gods"), Achilles slaughters the Trojans, filling the rivers with blood and dead bodies; eventually he kills Hector in front of the Scaean gate, binds his feet to the chariot with leather thongs and drags the body to the Greek camp, where he keeps defiling him. He then proceeds to the funeral of Patroclus and sacrifices on the pyre "many noble sheep and many sleek cattle" and four horses and two dogs. "And twelve noble sons of the great-hearted Trojans he slaughtered with the bronze."[5] Despite all these sacrificial victims (or possibly because of them?) the pyre does not kindle; only the intervention of another goddess—the fifth one[6]—will allow for Achilles' task to succeed.

The proximate famous cause for Achilles' second wave of "strife and rage" is the killing of Patroclus by the hands of Hector. Therefore, before tracing the psychodynamic path of this second phase of Achilles' wrath to its conclusion, it is crucial to take a detour and explore the figure of Patroclus, the keystone of the epic, whose death unbinds into action the rage of Achilles, which will cause the death of Hector and with him the destruction of Troy and the end of the free western Anatolian kingdoms with their shared culture.

THE ROLE OF PATROCLUS (BOOK XVI)

Who was Patroclus? And what were Homer's mental images out of which this figure and character took form?

Throughout the book Homer gives us a touching and respectful, attentive view of the son of Menoetius. From his descriptions, as well as in the mind and words of Achilles, during the three scenes that include him prior to Book XVI and his fatal aristeia, Patroclus, reportedly the older of the two, is alternatively the attendant,[7] companion, and shadow of Achilles: patient, quiet, always friendly, helpful,[8] and ready to obey Achilles' orders; always very close by, in an intimate relationship.[9] Homer encapsulated his character in the eulogy-like statement by Menelaus, while fighting over Patroclus' body: "Aiantes, leaders of the Argives, and you, Meriones, now let each man remember the kindliness of poor Patroclus, for to all was he ever gentle while he lived."[10]

Evidently Homer referred to material from the Epic Cycle in depicting Patroclus this way. The son of Menoetius is given very little relevance until book XI and then again Book XVI. He does not say a single word for sixteen books—the duration of the strife with Agamemnon—apart from a query to Achilles in Book XI (l. 606): "Why do you call me, Achilles? What need have you of me?" and being ordered to go to Nestor for information about a wounded Achaean, when he also shared a few words with the old king and with wounded Eurypylus.

He and Achilles have only two direct conversations, both controversial: the first when Achilles ridicules Patroclus' crying over the Achaeans' suffering, and Patroclus responds by harshly condemning Achilles' behavior; the second when the ghost of Patroclus denounces Achilles for having forgotten him and his burial, thus keeping him from passing through the gates of Hades, "beyond the river", and joining the world of the dead, where he could mingle with "the phantoms of men that have done with toils."[11] A very strange silence, between these two closest friends, during such a major crisis; a silence even more puzzling in the face of Nestor's words to Patroclus, in Book XI: ". . . you did Menoetius, son of Actor, thus charge: 'My child, in birth is Achilles nobler than you . . . but speak to him well a word of wisdom and give him counsel and direct him, and he will obey you to his profit.' Thus did the old man charge you, but you are forgetful."[12]

An intriguing dimension of this figure's symbolic function emerges if it is examined in the context of his psychic complementarity to Achilles, as Homer imagined and linked these two characters in his mind. To balance the impetuous, anger-ridden, battle-born, tragic narcissism of the dark hero figure, the poet used the older, patient, quiet, friendly and empathic cluster of the Patroclus-companion psychic configuration.[13]

He is the balanced component of the self, whose function may be to keep Achilles' explosive temperament under some sort of check, and to provide structure and meaningful direction to the cauldron of libidinal energy that constantly burns within the dark self-shadow of the son of Thetis.[14] In a Freudian structural landscape he would represent a wise ego/superego structure, able of heroic deeds himself, but for altruistic rather than narcissistic reasons, and invested in containing the destructiveness of the instinctual domain of the drives.

Patroclus (the name literally means "glory of the father"), was older than Achilles. He had experienced the power of unrestrained aggression when, a child himself, he had killed another child "over dice" and had to undergo purification by leaving the father's household, as was the custom of the times; he went to Peleus, who may have adopted him. He apparently developed a strong set of defensive operations against all unjustified expressions of the aggressive drive. These may have consisted at first in repression and reaction formation, which may cripple a child's personality, if used too early in life,[15] and later evolved in more mature forms as suppression and altruism. By the allusion to the childhood murder, Homer hints here at a psychodynamic element in Patroclus' development that will participate to his undoing.

A vivid metaphorical description of Achilles' psychic gestalt and its bipolarity is captured by Homer in Book XIX. When Briseis is returned to him, at the sight of dead Patroclus she "flung herself about him and shrieked aloud..." stating "so I wail you in your death and know no ceasing, for you were ever kind." "So she spoke weeping and to it the women added their laments; Patroclus indeed they mourned, but each one their own sorrows. But around Achilles gathered the elders of the Achaeans," to whom he states that "not at all would his heart be comforted until he entered the mouth of bloody war."[16] Homer depicted touchingly on one side the gentle, maternal Patroclus component, the hero white anima, surrounded by the feminine feeling function weeping for her own demise together with that of her hero-animus[17]; while on the other side stands the fierce and war-searching Achilles component, the dark animus, surrounded by archetypal derivatives of the masculine warrior/hero in a fully activated state. The scene calls to mind similar metaphors of the closely intertwined and interdependent masculine and feminine functions, as the Yang and the Yin, sun and moon, light and darkness.

Homer knows, though, that the situation has to change dramatically: the restraining, moderate Patroclus component of the combined self has to die. It is time for the epic to set up the conditions and antecedents required to cause the "unbinding of Ares," the death of Hector and the fall of the city. Therefore, stirred into action by the pressure of the grave and real danger to his ships raised by the Trojans, while still conflicted between his wrath and the fate of the Achaeans, the hero persona of Achilles responds to the intrapsychic conflict by splitting and by relinquishing to his alter Ego the role of the savior, of the one willing to put his own life on the line for the sake of the Achaeans.

(Ultimately, Achilles will not enter the fray to save anybody, but purely for revenge and glory.)

The gradual erosion and fragmentation of the Patroclus-Achilles gestalt is among the most compelling psychodynamic events of the entire poem, which also provides the psychological antecedents and the roots of this final episode of strife and wrath, and brings further clarity on Homer's feeling and thinking functions involved in the intuitive perceptions that fostered and colored the cognitive expression of his work.

The ambivalence and denial of Achilles toward this soft side of the self—a side that Homer will depict again in the scene of Briseis crying over dead Patroclus—is vividly captured in the words that Pelides uses against the tears of Patroclus who is hurting deeply at the sight of what has befallen upon the Greeks all over the camp. At no other time these two opposite sides of the gestalt emerge as clearly as now, and this moment deserves being revisited. It is also the first time, as mentioned, that Achilles and Patroclus talk directly to each other.

After attending to Eurypylus, Patroclus returns to the hut of Achilles shedding tears "like a fountain of dark water that down over the face of a sheer cliff pours its dusky stream."[18] Achilles does not try to console him, or to show concern for the cause of such anguish; rather, he distances himself psychically by using sarcasm and by criticizing Patroclus for his tears "like a girl, a mere babe, who runs to her mother's side and asks her to pick her up, and clutches at her gown and <u>hinders her in her going</u>..."[19]

Is this a description of how Achilles perceives their bond? Does he resent the soft, maternal archetypal derivative personified in Patroclus, and the stirring of guilt? Does he reveal the significant imbalance in the relationship, using the defense of sarcasm to trivialize the parental and nurturing, protective role activated and expressed by his friend's anguish? It is also telling that Achilles compares Patroclus not even to a baby boy but to a babe girl, highlighting the feminine function of this component of his psyche and the tension between these opposites. He clearly admits that this aspect of Patroclus "hinders" him in his going.[20]

Patroclus rebuffs Achilles vehemently. The most mature aspects of the Ego/superego structure, activated by witnessing the Achaean suffering, confront the Id derivatives in the first speech to Achilles since the beginning of the epic. Patroclus accuses Pelides of having caused vast suffering among the Achaeans with strong and condemning words: "you are impossible to deal with, Achilles. Never on me let such wrath lay hold, as the wrath you cherish, you whose valor causes harm! How will any other yet to be born have profit of you, if you do not ward off loathsome destruction from the Argives? Pitiless one, your father, it appears, was not the horseman Peleus, nor was Thetis your mother, but the gray sea bore you, and the sheer cliffs, since your mind is unbending."[21] He then presents the suggestion of Nestor: "grant me to buckle on my shoulder that armor of yours in the hope that the Trojans may take me for you."[22] Achilles revisits the cause of the strife—the prize woman Briseis taken away by Agamemnon—and decides that "these things will be let be as past and done" (emphasis mine). However, he still does not lead the Myrmidons but urges Patroclus to go and fight in his place, impersonating him by dressing his armor, so that the Trojans may not "burn the ships with blazing fire and take away our desired return."[23] At this point Homer has him give one last powerful command to his first lieutenant and closest friend; "But obey . . . so that you may win me great recompense and glory at the hands of all the Danaans, and that they send back that beauteous girl, and in addition give glorious gifts. When you have driven them from the ships, come back . . . (or) . . . you will lessen my honor."[24]

Patroclus initially follows the directives of his friend and commander: he pushes the Trojans away from the burning ship, extinguishes the fires, and drives the enemy from the camp and across the trench. Then in the mind of Homer this figure changes profoundly from the way he had been constantly perceived and described until now; for the first time in the Epic, he disobeys Achilles. The donning of Achilles' armor and identity, with their powerful dark symbolism, will convey more than his defensive system could contain. Patroclus will regress to the "game of dice" of childhood; the killing instinct will take over.

His identity still misrepresented and hidden by the armor, the more he wears it the more he gets corrupted into an imperfect copy of Pelides[25]; he falls under the dark influence of the Shadow; he crosses the trench, looking for Hector,[26] chases the Trojans and allies down the plain, and slays several Lycians among which their king, and son of Zeus, Sarpedon. Then, utterly disregarding the order of Achilles but becoming increasingly driven by blood lust and by hubris, he keeps pressing "after Trojans and Lycians, and was greatly blinded in heart. Fool that he was!"[27] and thrice he attempts to scale the walls of the city, each time being harshly repulsed by Apollo. However, unlike Achilles, who will fight with men and gods in his rampage, in utter disregard of either; or unlike Diomedes, who was allowed to fight, wound, and put to flight both Aphrodite and Ares; Patroclus cannot by constitution disrespect the gods. The spurious dark hero armor fades away, when faced with the divine. His softer, feminine side is revealed once more, and Hector thrusts his spear there, in the undefended lower belly, and kills him. His disobedience and death free Achilles' unbound rage and activate the gory rampage that follows his public reconciliation with Agamemnon and his request for the support of the Achaean army.

With the completion of the funeral for Patroclus the wrath at Hector continues through the defiling of his body. The mind of Achilles, deprived of the mitigating influence from his alter ego, is now driven primarily by emotional instability and rapidly changing moods. Even after the condemning judgement from all the gods of his ungodly behavior some of the enduring anger and of the curt, threatening insolence of Pelides is brought once more to the surface by Homer during the visit of Priam to the camp of the Myrmidons. To the request by the old king, a profoundly distraught and grieving father, to be allowed to receive at once the body of his son, Achilles angrily responds: "Do not provoke me further, old sir; I intend myself to give Hector back to you; for from Zeus there came to me a messenger (to do so) . . . and of you, Priam . . . some god led you.[28] . . . So now stir my heart no more among my sorrows, lest, old sir, I spare not even you inside my huts, my suppliant though you are."[29]

PSYCHODYNAMICS OF THE TRANSFERRED WRATH

The factors promoting the wrath of Achilles for Hector and everything Trojan carry a very different complexity than the ones discussed for the strife with Agamemnon and the Achaean army. They point to a primary intrapsychic nature of the conflict, and to projective regression as a protection from psychic anguish. The external causative factors in the confrontation with the Trojan new archenemy[30] are significantly minor when compared with those at the origin of the first strife, with its long life going back to Aulis and even to the first expedition.

That decades-long situation of covert tension, acrimony, and distrust between Achilles and Agamemnon is not present here. Achilles, as long as the Patroclus/Achilles gestalt is intact, has repeatedly demonstrated a very considerate attitude toward Hector, whom he describes as a powerful adversary—and he boasts about being the only one among the Achaeans able to keep Hector pinned near the city's walls, far from the ships—but not an enemy! He repeatedly states that he has no qualms against the Trojans, who fight for their women, their children, and their city. He was not a contender for the hand of "abhorred Helen"[31] and is not tied to the oath required by her father Tyndareus (although Patroclus was probably one of them[32] and bound by the oath). His role during the past nine years had been to plunder the towns of the Troad and nearby kingdoms, to capture slaves to either sell at markets like the one of Lesbos or to provide the Greek kings and chief warriors with concubines, and to keep Hector away from the ships.[33]

Then, Hector kills Patroclus. Achilles' intention to kill him in revenge is quite appropriate to the spirit of his time.[34] Hector must die, but the horrendous butchering and the furious defiling of his body are well beyond the external provocation. They indicate an intrapersonal destructive conflict of major proportions that requires externalization of the inner-directed guilt and rage through projection, in order for the damaged self to avoid self-annihilation.[35]

As reality sinks in, and he receives the news that Patroclus is dead, he is left with the realization that he has condemned his "better self" to die. His advice to Patroclus was steeped in narcissism rather than in concern for the other. It was not to protect him from dying that Achilles cautioned Patroclus to return after he pushed the Trojans back across the trench. The son of Menoetius may have died at any moment after leaving the relative security of the Myrmidons' huts and long before reaching the trench, as the experience of Vietnam survivors to the death of their closest buddies has demonstrated.[36] What Achilles seemed to be mainly concerned of was the possibility that Patroclus could kill Hector or even storm Troy, and deprive him of his glory, lessen his honor. Mostly, he appeared still unwilling to relent and take the lead in saving the Achaean army. The sending of Patroclus—actually, not even that: he simply agreed to Patroclus' request—was the best compromise he could reach between his stubborn anger and his fear for the fate of his ships in case of a complete Trojan victory.

His guilt transpires in his statement to his mother: "I was not to protect my comrade and his slaying. Far from his own land he has fallen, and had need of me to be a warder off of ruin."[37] These words will be closely repeated from another Vietnam soldier: "I didn't do my job, I didn't bring him home. . . . When it come the time. . . . I didn't take care of him. When he needed me, I wasn't there."[38]

For a brief moment Achilles is grieving his friend while facing his own profound guilt, and Homer captures with great empathy the acute pain from such a grievous loss. But quickly the psychic effects of the loss that left a broken Pelides[39] emerge: regression to primitive rage and to projection are activated,[40] and all his pain is cast in an inflated manner upon the ultimate target of the projection: Hector and every single Trojan.

With the death of Patroclus, the dynamics directing the wrath of Achilles shift from the expression of an interpersonal conflict to a fundamentally intrapersonal, or intrapsychic, one. Here one finds the real, deep tragedy of Achilles' fate: the pressure from overwhelming grief, guilt, and rage, the progressive decay of his Self by the silencing of the Ego and

Superego mediators, and the disinhibition of more primitive libidinal energies and archetypal derivatives.

At his very core, Achilles is left with the enduring self-condemnation that he sent his closest friend—his buddy in modern jargon—to die in his place, and the torturing thought that he should have been the one to lead the Myrmidons, and could have saved him.

HOMER AND THE ARISTEIA OF ACHILLES

Volumes have probably been written on the aristeia of Achilles. By Book XX we have been exposed to many battle descriptions, reflecting the standard Iliadic module: masses of foot soldiers face each other, "in close combat," or separated by a space "as wide as the throw of a javelin"; and often in that space the warriors/heroes—either in their chariots or by foot, their chariots and charioteers standing behind them—come out of the throngs of soldiers to challenge each other with words and with spears, and retreat back within the relative safety of all those bodies when they lose heart. Standing on their chariots, well above the mass of the foot soldiers, they can supervise the course of the battle, the location of the enemy leaders, and use the chariots to move rapidly where they perceive that their support is most needed. The armies of foot soldiers are always a steady background to their commanders, a presence that the reader perceives as deeply embedded in the landscape, the cast supporting the exploits of its heroes. Throughout the rest of the Epic, including the aristeia of Patroclus, Homer is very gifted in depicting a Scamander plain alive with moving and clamoring waves of anonymous armies, the soldiers briefly regaining their humanity when gathered among the fallen during the truces for the burning of the dead.

Homer opens Book XX with a similar scenario. With a great amount of divine noise "thus did the blessed gods urge the two armies to clash in battle."[41] "The whole plain was filled with men and horses and aflame with bronze . . . and two warriors best by far of all came together in the space between the two armies eager to do battle, Aeneas, Anchises' son, and noble Achilles."[42] Achilles tells Aeneas "to retreat back into the mass of men and stand not to face me"[43]; Aeneas responds in tone, comparing lineages; they both cast their spears, Poseidon saves Aeneas by lifting him "over many ranks of warriors and many chariots (to) where the Caucones were arming for war."[44] Achilles calls the Achaeans to join forces with him because, even if mighty, he could not fight the Trojans alone.[45] After a first encounter with Hector, during which Athene stops Hector's spear and Apollo snatches Hector to safety, the slaughter begins, and by the end of Book XX Achilles has killed fourteen named warriors, by spear or sword, and by then it feels as if Homer is beginning to move into a different scenario, a different dimension: the Achaean and the Trojan armies seem to gradually dissolve into nothingness. He still suggests their ongoing presence at the opening of Book XXI, at the ford of the Xanthus (the old name of the Scamander), where "Achilles split them into two groups, and one he drove to the plain toward the city . . . but half were forced into the deep-flowing river with its silver eddies . . . so before Achilles was the sounding stream of deep-eddying Xanthus filled with chariots and men in confusion."[46] The center stage, rich in movement and dramatic energy, is now where the Trojans who were unable to negotiate the congestion at the ford seek an escape from Achilles—and certainly from his Myrmidons, almost as eager as their king to revenge Patroclus—by jumping into the river and trying to cross it, frantically thrashing around in the deep waters of the Xanthus, as they flee from Pelides' killing rage. At the periphery of this central scene, in the landscape beyond the ford, two armies are sketched fading rapidly in the distance: the Trojans who were able to ford the river, and the victorious Danaans who had joined Achilles in the charge through the plain and to the ford, and are chasing them toward the city. Interestingly, and not like any other aristeia or battle episode, no Greek heroes are mentioned for the entire length of this last warring scene, until the action returns to the Greek camp and the ships. Even Agamemnon seems to have relinquished, in this last Iliadic battle, the scepter of command and has faded into anonymity. As I pointed out earlier on, Homer provides Achilles with exclusive leadership during these last scenes of untamed slaughter, and with the everlasting glory from his final act on the battleground, the ultimate divine reason for his existence: the death of Hector. The poet also charges him, however, with the sole responsibility for the gory slaying. No other Greek hero will participate to such a bloodbath.

The events with their related dynamics depicted in the main stage are built around the sole figure of the son of Peleus, who has also jumped in the Scamander and slaughters unnamed Trojans "until his hand grew weary"; then he "chose twelve youths alive out of the river as blood price for dead Patroclus, son of Menoetius. These he led out dazed like fawns, and bound their hands behind them with shapely throngs, which they themselves wore about their pliant tunics, and <u>gave them to his comrades</u> to take to the hollow ships."[47]

He kills a son of Priam, unarmed Lycaon. This killing scene goes on for one hundred verses, between pleads and dismissive responses; we are told that Achilles had already captured him, earlier on, and sold him to Lesbos for the equivalent of one hundred oxen; now he could get much more from Priam. Achilles confirms that before the death of Patroclus he preferred to capture Trojans and sell them as slaves in Lesbos, rather that kill them; but now he has no pity nor financial interests![48]

He then turns against Asteropeus, leader of the Paeonians, and kills him at the end of an encounter during which he asks for the lineage (and receives a grazing wound at the right forearm). And then he goes "after the Paeonians, lords of chariots, who were still huddled along the eddying river" and kills seven of them, "'and still more of the Paeonians would swift Achilles have slain if the deep-eddying river had not grown angry."[49]

Homer now resorts to capturing images of a landscape that has changed in a dramatic way. After Achilles dismisses the request of the river god Xanthus to stop defiling his waters with blood and death, the entire Scamander plain becomes flooded by the angry river who casts all the dead bodies out of his bed and on the land[50] while "the living he saved under his fair streams, hiding them in eddies deep and wide."[51] No one else but Achilles is described trying to flee from the chasing waters, fearful for his life. No one. Not even his faithful Myrmidons and their five, carefully selected leaders of whom "he himself in his great might was lord over all."[52] Where are they?

Homer has moved the tragedy to the dimension of the divine; the entire theater is reorganized to play out the context between the gods. Achilles tries repeatedly and unsuccessfully to take a stand against the divine power, only to have each time to flee again, "distressed at heart"; until he turns in anguish to Zeus, praying that his life be spared from a drowning death. Zeus is silent but four gods come in succession to support Pelides, particularly Hera, who snatches Achilles from certain drowning (now the Simois river has joined his brother!) by unleashing her son Hephaestus against the rivers.

Homer orchestrates here yet another capturing image of a Scamander plain still void of the human element—even Achilles falls briefly by the sidelines—but becoming the center stage for the battle between the gods. Hephaestus "made ready wondrous blazing fire," and the "whole plain dried, and the dead he utterly consumed; and then against the river he turned his gleaming flame."[53] Homer evokes for us a torched and lifeless plain, littered with burnt corpses, and a raging fire along the riverbanks, engulfing all vegetation and the river itself.[54] It is a deadly, violent battle between the two basic elements and opposites, water and fire, who fight to either subdue the enraged psychic configuration of Achilles by literally drowning and burying it down deep (within the symbiotic engulfment of the water, a mother-womb image?); or to reinforce with divine energy his desire for vengeance and killing.[55] Pelides will eventually reappear through the eyes of Priam, "huge, and... before him the Trojans were being driven in headlong rout."[56] Until that moment, though, Homer keeps the landscape exclusively for the use of the gods: stirred by the serious fight between Xanthus and Hephaestus, the pro-Trojans and pro-Greeks factions of the Immortals descend onto the plain and confront each other in the rather ineffectual "battle of the gods."

Then Homer returns to the human landscape, and the scene moves to the Scaean gates and to the plain in front of them, beyond the ford and on the other side of the river. The poet closes Book XXI by concocting the disguise trick played by Apollo who will distract Achilles away in a futile chase, and thus allow the Trojans to stream inside the city. The stage is set for the next chapter: a locked city, an Achilles running far away from its serrated gates, and—we will soon learn—a conflicted Hector standing close to them.

For the present analysis, the interest concerning the history-making duel will be articulated around what Homer experiences and reveals as he enters the personas of the protagonists and becomes effectively enmeshed in the happenings.

When so absorbed, his feelings come to life and color the descriptive layer with their unique nuances. He exploits those moments to convey persuasive messages through comparisons and innuendos. An example of this skill is presented at the beginning of Book XXII. After looking through the eyes of Priam at the onrushing Achilles, similar to the star Sirius,[57] Homer enters the character of Hector in a series of affectively rich images. The Trojan prince stands, alone, just outside of the barred Scaean Gates, watching the distant Achilles rushing toward him. On top of the wall his parents implore him to enter the city and save himself, Priam with ominous predictions of his own fate, Hecabe proffering her naked breast (the only time Homer describes such a highly symbolic act). Hector is deeply ridden with guilt for having caused so much suffering and death to the Trojans and allies; filled with shame, he could not face the Trojan women grieving their dead ones, nor the reproach of Polydamas, whose wise counsel to retreat into the city he had discarded. It is important to revisit what Homer imagined to be going through the mind of Hector, as he faced the consequences of his stubborn arrogance and of his retaliatory rage at the invading Achaeans, and the dismissal of his friend's pleas: "Ah, me, if I go inside the gates and the walls, Polydamas will be the first to put reproach on me, since he told me to lead the Trojans to the city. . . . But now, since I have brought the army to ruin through my blind folly, I feel shame before the Trojans, and the Trojans' wives with trailing robes, lest perhaps some baser than I, may say: "Hector, trusting in his own might, brought ruin to the army. . . but for me it would be far better to meet Achilles."

The poet creates a distinct contrast, here, with what he imagined Achilles would say when he recognized the grievous error from his rage: "Son of Atreus . . . we raged in soul-devouring strife for the sake of a girl? I wish that among the ships Artemis had slain her with an arrow. . . . Then not so many Achaeans would have bitten the vast earth with their teeth . . . because of the fierceness of my wrath. . . . But these things will be let be, as past and done. . . . Now I end my wrath. But come, rouse up speedily the long-haired Achaeans to battle, so that I may go out against the Trojans."

One does not hear, in the words of Achilles, any trace of the personal guilt and shame, of the deep regret for all the dead and for their wives, and of not feeling worth to join them again (unless he killed their nemesis or died in the attempt), that one finds in Hector. Apart from the "biting the dust" comment, Achilles' main concern for the Achaeans is that they go back to fight at once (Odysseus will eventually convince him to allow the soldiers some rest and food, before sending them back into combat), so that he could seek his revenge.

The drama then runs, quite literally, to its preordained completion. As Homer recreates these last scenes that encapsulate the peak moments of the entire epic, he is quite aware of the historically obligated outcome, the killing of Hector by Achilles. In his imagination he comes up, though, with those famous three laps around the city. While one observes, through Homer's eyes, the desperate flight of Hector along the walls of Troy—which recalls the equally desperate flight of Achilles on the Scamander plain—chased by Pelides,[58] the visuals are accompanied by a string of comments[59] with which the poet seems to call attention on the why's and how's surrounding the killing of Hector. He dies because his piety and the grief that Zeus feels for him[60] are overruled by the writings of Fate—a power that not even the gods can control—and by Athene's bitter search for revenge.[61] Homer is attentive in reminding the audiences that Hector dies because the gods ultimately either abandoned him—Zeus and Apollo—or actively deceived him and played a crucial role in his death—as Athene.[62]

Achilles kills him with the famous Pelian spear that Athene has retrieved after he, although the "best of the Achaeans," has actually missed the throw, while the cast of Hector was perfect, but the shield of Hephaestus was impenetrable. Why did Homer make Achilles visibly the lesser of the two in the context with the spears? He then describes how Hector, without a second spear—and without a fake brother!—charges brandishing his sword, but Achilles picks up his Pelian spear and kills him. Why didn't the poet offer Achilles a second chance of besting Hector in a fair fight with swords, rather than through the deceptions of a goddess?[63] The duel is very brief, but the way Homer describes its unfolding carries a less than laudatory meaning for Pelides.

Much has also been written on the statement of Achilles to the dying Hector: "I wish that somehow wrath and fury might drive me to carve your flesh and myself eat it raw."[64] These writings—modern interpretations and/or revisions of the ancient Homeric text—involve the meanings given to the cannibalistic images that one encounters in the *Iliad* and that are usually considered expressions of a significantly abnormal and diseased psychic system, as well as indexes of significant loss in the subject of the sense of self as a human being. The characterization of the behavior of Achilles in Books XXI and XXII as a berserk condition is significantly based on this psychological regression to a non-human level.

Were indeed these purely imagined wishes the expressions of the psychic regression decried by our collective psychic system, to be seen as major aberrations from the collective spirit of Homeric humans, or rather predictable imaginal fantasies, foreseeable psychoemotional responses to specific affective states? Achilles clearly implies that the level of his actual "wrath and fury" is not sufficient to transform the wish into an action.

I was not in the world of Homer, embedded and part of that sociocultural milieu, and therefore I am blind as to what these images meant to the mind of the poet. My analysis is limited to the observable facts, and I observed that in the *Iliad* the images were present—and therefore admissible—at the highest level of the culture's collective superego: Homer has Zeus attribute them to his wife Hera in Book IV, ll.34 ff.: "Strange queen . . . if you were to enter inside the gates and the high walls and to devour Priam raw and the sons of Priam and all the Trojans besides, then perhaps you might heal your anger." It should not surprise, then, if this divine response to high distress was shared by a Priam and an Achilles, and even an Hecabe![65] Indeed, the fantasies in the humans required significantly greater and emotionally devastating stimuli—loss and grief—than the divine one—jealousy for a beauty prize given to another contender by an adolescent shepherd who was a predestined pawn to the machinations of the Godhead.

Psychology teaches us about the great difference between impulse and action. The complex domain of instinctual drives, the Id of the Freudian structural model, is filled with potent oral aggressive wishes that may, or may not, percolate upwards to invest the domain of Ego consciousness without being necessarily translated into actions.[66] In Homeric times it seems these fantasies were more easily acknowledged as part of the collective human psychic landscape, and of the divine one as well.

Furthermore, the psychological mechanisms involved in (ritual) cannibalism may be more complex than simple regressive loss of the subject's identity. Rather, the role played by essentialism may be a strong catalyst for the regression of the Other—the anti-Self—to a non-human level (this being the basic psychological mechanism activating the modern terrorist), and eating "it" can be perceived as the ultimate confirmation of its animal state.

With the death of Hector, the aristeia of Achilles is completed but the wrath continues. Before revisiting its last phase, though, I will briefly discuss the aristeia itself, which is possibly the highest and most significant[67] testimony to Achilles being "the best of the Achaeans."

What characterizes a successful combat exploit? Dr. Shay—and scores of written reports since the times of the Great Pharaoh—points to the importance of the "body count": how many where killed in the action.

When we analyze the aristeia of Patroclus we come up with a count of fifty-four Trojans and Lycians killed; the body count for Achilles is of thirty-six, of which twenty-four were killed in action, while twelve youth were captured and will be sacrificed on the pyre of Patroclus.[68] There are more: the ones slaughtered in the river "until his hands got weary," but

Homer uncharacteristically does not tell us how many. Compare this with the similar description of how Patroclus "thrice he leapt on them, the peer of swift Ares, crying a terrible cry, and thrice he slew nine men."[69]

Once more one's attention is turned to what is not said, followed by an attempt to decipher the why. Homer is keenly aware of the importance of body counts and of the standing of each victim, as indicated by the accurate listing and the almost universal insertion of various details about each contender. It is odd that in this particular occasion, given the very high stakes tied to his reports, he would fail to use the same formula that he used for Patroclus: he could easily have enriched the description of how Achilles leapt on the Trojans and slew them in the deep eddies and along the banks, by adding something along the line: "four scores he killed, and then his hands grew tired." A scene like that, colored by the skills of the poet, would have sealed the primacy of Pelides as "aristos" among the Achaeans. Instead, the poet lets the audience decide the extent of his prowess in battle.

HECTOR, ACHILLES, AND PRIAM

The next stage of Achilles' wrath, now expressed against dead Hector, begins also in front of the locked city. The naked body of the Trojan Prince is stretched on the ground and is repeatedly stabbed by the Achaeans, each one accompanying the act with some debasing remark. Then Achilles, as mentioned, pierced both Hector's feet "from knee to ankle and fastened through them thongs of oxhide, and bound them to his chariot, but left the head to trail behind,"[70] and dragged the body to the Achaean camp. "So was his head all befouled by dust."[71]

Homer then shifts the attention of the audience away from what is happening outside the walls and enters the city. For over one hundred lines the poet describes the widespread lamenting of all the Trojans; around the desperate parents "the people were given over to wailing and groaning throughout the city."[72] (Homer here evokes and anticipates, by a brief simile gravid with meaning, the major wailing and crying that will accompany the burning of the city as it will be destroyed by fire shortly after the death of Hector.[73])

The level of intensity expressed by Homer in the pain of Hecabe and Priam recalls that of Achilles at the sight of Patroclus' dead and naked body, with the same manifestations of grief: the groaning and the "groveling in the filth," the laying outstretched in the dust and the tearing of hair, the need to hold back Achilles' hands as well as frenzied Priam. We hear how the acute grief of the city is driven by a deep sense of loss for someone who was always greeted as a god and a very great glory, and a help to all; and the frantic despair of Priam is enhanced by the defiling of his son's body and by his religious need to offer Hector a proper burial; while the grief of Achilles from the profound loss is tinged, as we have observed, with equally profound guilt and with vindictive projected rage.[74]

Then Homer introduces the deeply touching figure of Andromache. He brings vividly to life her dreadful premonition that makes "my heart leaps to my mouth, and beneath me my knees are numbed," and her fainting at the sight of her husband dragged toward the Greek camp. And he concludes with Andromache's heart-rending lament on the fate of their son. Even if he escapes with his life from the Achaeans—he will not; he will be thrown down from the walls either by Odysseus, or by Achilles' son, Neoptolemus—he will live as an orphan child, "cut off from the friends of his youth . . . his head bowed low . . . his cheeks bathed in tears," and shunned by his father's friends, until "in tears to his widowed mother comes back the child."[75]

While the description of Andromache's somatic expressions of acute anxiety indicates Homer's empathic inter-subjective sharing with her mental state, his detailed lines about the fate of an orphan may reflect something more private, and perhaps speak of a shared personal experience of orphanhood. The accounts of the violent death of Astyanax, Hector's son and potential heir, were certainly repeatedly reported and discussed among the sad sagas of the times, as an example of particularly brutal Greek vengeance. If, indeed, there is a kernel of truth in the reports about the origins of Homer, the illegitimate pregnancy and his status as a fatherless child, one has to wander how those gruesome stories about the Trojan prince affected his infantile mind and contributed to empathic identification with Astyanax and to his reactions toward the Greek callous and violent ways in handling anything and anyone who was not of their liking, Achilles being the prototypical example of such self-centered violence.

The scene then returns to the Greek camp and to an Achilles who continues to defile the body of Hector while performing the gory funeral of Patroclus—and Homer points to how the pyre would not have kindled without the intercession of the four god winds—and organizing the funeral games.

Eventually the gods decry their revulsion for his impious treatment of a dead; Zeus orders Achilles to stop and to relinquish the body of Hector to his father, and sends Hermes to safely guide Priam to the hut of Pelides. Achilles appears to finally relent in his wrath; he genuinely cries at the sight and words of Priam, who brings back memories of his own father Peleus.

But Homer has been invested with this character too long not to perceive and absorb, so to speak, the radical change in the psychic organization of Achilles that followed the loss of his "half-twin", of the stabilizing alter ego of Patroclus. The mood of Pelides appears to cycle rapidly, subject to the unfiltered reception of the surrounding emotional landscape. Concurrently, he appears unable to hold within his psyche any distressing situation of tension and conflict, and he cannot handle psychic pain for too long without a reactivation of his narcissistic defenses, like externalization of the dysphoric state, counter aggression, and defiant refusal/denial of any external and internal constraints. The parenthesis of sharing with the old king the pain that results from a loss is filled with great intensity, but it is also rather brief and one-sided.[76] His activation of the repressive mechanism is externalized also in his advice to Priam: "do not grieve ever ceaselessly in your heart; for nothing will you accomplish by grieving for your son"; he seems to imply that grieving, as his for Patroclus, is useless unless one gets the grieved one back. When Priam keeps the wound open by refusing to sit down[77] and insisting in being allowed to see his son ("give him back quickly, so that my eyes may look on him") the anger of Achilles emerges again. He will return the body of Hector because the gods have required it and clearly a god accompanied Priam, but he is doing it under divine duress; Priam's insistence is another provocation and he does not intend to submit to human pressure. Therefore, the threat: "Do not provoke me further, old sir . . . stir my heart no more among my sorrows, lest, old sir, I spare not even you inside the huts, my suppliant though you are, and so transgress the charge of Zeus."

Priam desists and with it the wrath dissipates. Achilles has his attendants clean and anoint Hector, and with them he puts the body on the wagon, while keeping all this activity out of Priam's sight, in order to avoid stirring Priam to another emotional surge, afraid of what his own actions would be, if faced with more distress.[78] Overall, though, the strife has come to a conclusion and he will even negotiate a truce for the Trojans to be able and offer Hector a proper funeral; eventually he retires to his bed, "and by his side lay fair-cheeked Briseis."

The analysis of these last events casts also a bridge across the entire epic and the themes addressed by the opening lines. Homer, in what is possibly the most significant of his several mirroring of specific scenes, reframes in the epilogue the prologue of his epic. I am referring to the symmetry between Book I and Book XXIV, only partially obscured by the length of the intervening narrative and by the overt difference in situations and characters.

In both books Homer presents the extent of Greek wrath and Greek impiety, which repels and offends the divine dimension. The impiety of Agamemnon against Chryses at the beginning of the epic finds its echo, at the end of it, in the impiety of Achilles toward the body of Hector and his threat of further impiety by killing Priam and defying the demand of Zeus. Both situations are articulated around the compelling figure of a father, walking into the Greek enemy camp to ransom his child; the quest of both fathers needing the intervention of a god in order to have the child returned to them.

The deeply touching figures of the two Trojan fathers—Chryses and Priam—have great similarities in their intense sorrow and longing for their children and in their daring efforts to rescue them: either a daughter, her living body bound to be sexually despoiled; or a son, his dead body dragged and ravaged in the dust; and both fathers are exposed, in presenting their requests of ransom, to Greek anger and threats of severe beatings (Agamemnon) or even death (Achilles). It is difficult, for an analyst, not to ponder on the psychic processes in Homer's mind that brought him to select the debasement of a human being of either sex, expressed through the symbolisms of their bodies, as a most serious impious sin calling for harsh divine punishment: the woman's body defiled through collective murder, slavery, and rape; the man's body through physical mauling and defacement out of collective violence, vindictiveness and rage. Homer seemed to capture and condemn the perennial dark side of the male archetype, expressed in sexually differentiated forms but equally destructive of the object's psychological identity. These two figures—the woman and the man—remain connected, at the two ends of the *Iliad* and across the entire length of it, by the repeatedly played out themes of men killing men, and women being prized part of the pillaging as enslaved sexual objects.

The similarity between the opening and the closing scenes is certainly not casual; rather, it strongly suggests a grand design, long in the planning and in its completion. Homer appears to bring back to the surface the enduring quality of the two significant themes that he identified in the first seven lines of the *Iliad*. Both themes—the wrath of Achilles and the relationship with the divine—touch us once more, full force, at the end of the poem; they have never found closure but have continued to run throughout the entire narrative, as the *Iliad* kept unfolding around what emerges as the principal cause of its existence: the fate of Hector upon which rests in balance the fate of the region.

By bringing back into evidence the two central themes Homer brought also into light the existence of paths linking the opening and closing scenes of each theme and running through the entire epic. A path for each theme, at times visible, at times obscure, connects dispersed occurrences and reminders of anger and greed, piety and impiety, which provide data about the collective psyche in the Greek and the Trojan camps as well as about the psychodynamics of distinct individuals, but principally of the poet himself.

NOTES

1. "... when Achilles saw the arms, then wrath came on him still more, and his eyes showed forth terribly from beneath their lids, like flame" *Iliad*, Book XIX, ll. 15 ff. The armor, cast in the fire of the crippled god, seems to represent a powerful symbol of psychic inflation of the Shadow, the dark, malevolent side of the hero figure.

2. Ibid., ll. 56 ff.

3. A few hours earlier Thetis had described to Hephaestus how her son had been wasting his heart in grief of her. Once more, Achilles grief, in the words and mind of Homer, appears to be deeply vindictive and deadly.

4. Ibid., ll. 67 ff.

5. *Iliad*, Book XXIII, ll. 165 ff.

6. Athene (in Books I and Book XXI at the Scaean gate); Thetis; Hera, when the god-river Scamander is close to drown him to the sea; and now Iris.

7. Dr. Shay preferentially uses the term therapon and translates it as "second in command," but Homer uses this term in the plural to describe Achilles' attendants (XXIV, l. 573), one of its many meanings (other ones being servant, slave, worshipper, comrade, aid).... The poet describes Patroclus also as ("polu philtatos" far the dearest) hetairos (XI l. 602, XVII l. 411, XVIII l. 81). Homer usually uses hetaîros as companion, or comrade, for soldiers under the same commander.

8. Homer depicts this side of Patroclus quite touchingly throughout Book XI when, ordered by Achilles, he goes to the hut of Nestor and then assists the wounded Eurypylus. During this journey into the conflict and pain of the Achaean army he receives from Nestor, the wise patriarch, the initial suggestion to disguise himself as an Achilles; a fatal suggestion!

9. The relationship between these two figures has been subject to multiple interpretations, including the sexual one by later Greek figures as Aeschylus and Phaedrus. In the *Iliad* the only direct allusion to their sexuality is found when Homer describes how Achilles "slept in the innermost part of the well-built hut, and by his side lay a woman he had brought from Lesbos ... fair-cheeked Diomede. And Patroclus lay down on the opposite side, and by him likewise lay fair-belted Iphis, whom noble Achilles had given him when he took steep Scyrus, the city of Enyeus." (*Iliad*, Book IX, ll. 663 ff.): one finds the only allusion to physical intimacy between the two in the plead of Achilles to the ghost of Patroclus: "But come closer, though it may be but for a little time, let us clasp our arms about one another, and take our fill of dire lamenting." (*Iliad*, Book XXIII, ll. 97-98). Finally, during a touching description of Pelides mournfully recalling memories of his friend, Homer describes Achilles as "yearning for the manhood and valiant might of Patroclus..." (*Iliad*, Book XXIV, ll. 5 ff.)

10. *Iliad*, Book XVII, ll. 669 ff.

11. *Iliad*, Book XXIII, ll. 71 ff.

12. *Iliad*, Book XI, ll. 785 ff.

13. Shay describes modern derivatives of this archetypal dyadic gestalt among Vietnam soldiers: "the twin-like closeness that the two soldiers shared, a closeness that allowed them to feel that each was the other double." (Shay, p. 70).

14. She actually did put him in the fire, as a baby, as we have seen (Argonautica 4:869-879).

15. Beardslee et al., p. 177.

16. *Iliad*, Book XIX, ll. 282 ff.

17. Jung considers the anima and the animus as fundamental anthropomorphic archetypes of the collective unconscious mind, transcending the personal psyche. The animus represents the unconscious masculine side of a woman, and the anima represents the unconscious feminine side of a man. As with all the other archetypal functions, they exist in two opposite configurations.

18. A simile that Homer uses only another time, and for a similar situation, to describe the feelings of Agamemnon when faced with the suffering of his army (Book IX, ll. 13 ff).

19. *Iliad*, Book XVI, ll. 7 ff. (emphasis mine).

20. The domain of the drives—the id—is hindered in its expression and gratification by the defensive systems set up by the Ego and Superego.

21. *Iliad*, Book XVI, ll. 29 ff. The Ego/Superego system recognizes the prehuman sources of the instinctual domain. There is also a metaphorical suggestion of an alchemical experiment, a forced conjunction between opposing elements of "prima materia."

22. Ibid., ll. 40 ff. Homer adds at this point: "so he spoke in prayer, great fool that he was, for it was certain to be his own evil death and fate for which he prayed." It is not a mystery to the audiences that Patroclus will die. It was not even a mystery to Achilles: Thetis had mentioned it, without making names but her description was fairly clear. One has the impression that Homer wanted to remind Patroclus' fate once more, immediately preceding Achilles sending him to his death. In psychological terms it also implies that by shifting his identity to the one of Achilles—by allowing the id to colonize the Ego and the Superego—Patroclus signs his own psychic death warrant.

23. Ibid., ll. 81 ff. Achilles is now clearly talking about his ships being in danger. Still, he does not lead his forces, contrary to his statements to Odysseus and Aias.

24. Ibid., ll. 83 ff.

25. From the perspective of depth psychology, we observe a regression of Achilles' alter ego under the onslaught of the dark hero persona. As Homer knows well, Patroclus has since childhood carried within himself the shadowy experience of killing from explosive rage. This potent "attractor"—to use the term by A. Scott—had been contained and inactivated through repression and reaction formation to the opposite, super gentle persona. When he is ordered to carry Achilles' armor on his shoulders, and in his psyche, the adaptive defensive system erected as a boundary through the "purification" process becomes progressively blurred and the repressed murderous shadow—and its destructive libidinal charge—finds its way back in the open. By attempting to absorb its dark energy, to dress the armor, the true Patroclus is left increasingly vulnerable to an existential psychic conflict and to psychic annihilation. The developmental theme described earlier allows for a more in-depth understanding of his psychic struggle.

26. "Against Hector did the heart of Patroclus urge him on, for he was eager to strike him" *Iliad*, Book XVI, ll. 381-382. An anticipation and prelude of Achilles' main objective.

27. *Iliad*, Book XVI, ll. 685 ff.

28. Achilles admits awareness of how involved the gods are in the case, but he submits grudgingly, reluctantly, to the divine request.

29. *Iliad*, Book XXIV, ll. 560 ff.

30. It may have been essayist Norman Bergen who suggested the existence of a powerful human need to contain evil within the self—in order to avoid complete inflation and fragmentation of the Ego (the ego cannot contain the unbound evil archetype)—by assigning (projecting) it to a specific event or person, as Hector in the case of Achilles. Such a defensive maneuver is naturally bound to fail in that the boundary between the original subject and the projected components of the evil is permeable at best, even if at all present.

31. *Iliad*, Book XIX, l. 325: "for the sake of abhorred Helen am warring with the men of Troy."

32. His name appears in the listings of suitors compiled by Pseudo-Apollodorus and Hyginus.

33. Andromache, though, dispels some of this restrained image of Achilles by reminding how he killed her father and her seven brothers, and released her mother only after he had received "ransom past counting" (*Iliad*, Book VI, ll. 413 ff.). Priam also laments that Achilles has already killed many of his sons (*Iliad*, Book XXII, ll. 45 ff.) and we heard Briseis lamenting her losses.

34. The death penalty for grievous behavior is still a legal retribution in our times, a reflection of the cultural evolution and level of psychological maturity—or lack of it—among diverse social systems through three millennia.

35. In the only example cited in the *Iliad* of destructiveness turned against the self, Homer has Antilochus hold the hands of Achilles, after he informed Pelides of Patroclus' death, "for he feared that he might cut his throat with the knife." (*Iliad*, Book XVIII, ll. 32 ff.)

36. "And [he]'s is probably 15 feet away [from me]. And when he jumped . . . he jumped on a mine. And there was nothing left of him" (Shay, p. 71).

37. *Iliad*, Book XVIII, ll. 98 ff.

38. Shay, p. 69.

39. ". . . the death of a special friend-in-arms broke the survivor's life into unhealable halves." (Shay, p. 39).

40. Splitting—either of self or of other images—projection, repression and denial of affect with reaction formation, and derogatory devaluation, are among the immature or primitive defensive mechanisms of the narcissistic personality disorder.

41. *Iliad*, Book XX, l. 54.

42. Ibid., ll. 156 ff.

43. Ibid., l. 196-197.

44. Ibid., ll. 325 ff.

45. He spoke, and leapt along the ranks and called to each man: "No longer now stand far from the Trojans, noble Achaeans, but come, let man go out against man. . . . Hard it is for me, even though I am mighty, to deal with so many men and to fight them all." *Iliad*, Book XX, ll. 353 ff.

46. *Iliad*, Book XXI, ll. 1 ff.

47. *Iliad*, Book XXI, ll. 26 ff.(emphasis mine).

48. All these instances, from his addressing the army to the conversation with Aeneas, to the first encounter with Hector, to the tying up of the twelve youths and giving them in charge of his comrades, to his fleeing the river and asking for help from the gods, and finally to his dialogue with Hector in Book XXII, indicate that in the mind of Homer Achilles is not operating in a berserk condition. He is highly vindictive and trying to obliterate his guilt through projection and revenge, but he is cool-headed in his seeking revenge, in full command of all his senses. He had previously described to dead Patroclus what his behavior will be, and he sticks carefully to his script.

49. *Iliad*, Book XXI, ll. 209 ff.

50. "and the whole plain was filled with a flood of water, and many fair weapons of young men slain in battle were floating there, along with their corpses." *Iliad*, ibid., ll. 298 ff.

51. Ibid., ll. 235 ff.

52. *Iliad*, Book XXVI, l. 172.

53. *Iliad*, Book XXI, ll. 342 ff.

54. "so burned in fire his fair streams, and the water boiled" Ibid., ll. 364-365.

55. Hephaestus had also given him the new armor, forged in the same divine fire, just a few hours before.

56. Ibid., ll. 526 ff.

57. The meaning of this simile was well documented already in Homeric times and therefore less susceptible to revisionism from different spirits of different sociocultural eras. Sirius, the brightest star in the summer morning sky (and therefore present during that fatidic summer), is part of the constellation of the Greater Dog (Canis Major); ancient lore has it that this was originally the dog donated by the Goddess Eos to her mortal lover Cephalus, and subsequently raised to the Heavens by Zeus because of its unparalleled speed. Once there, it has been hunting for Orion and helping him to fight the great Bull (Taurus). It is probably the same star "of harvest time, that shines brightest of all others" to which Homer compares Diomedes after Athene has "kindled from his helmet and shield flame unwearying" (Book V, ll. 4 ff.); the likes of what she did with Achilles as he starts his campaign. Or the one that the poet uses for

Hector: "as for among the clouds there gleams the destructive star...so Hector would appear among the foremost..." (*Iliad*, Book XI, ll. 62 ff.)

58. "In front a good man fled, but one far better pursued him swiftly; ... it was for the life of horse-taming Hector that they ran." This is Zeus' comment, while the gods watch the race. *Iliad*, Book XXII, ll. 158 ff.

59. Among these there is the interesting report of a dream of chasing and being chased that appears to be a personal disclosure, given the lack of any named dreamer! "And as in a dream a man cannot pursue one who flees before him—the one can not flee, nor the other pursue..." (Ibid. ll. 199 ff.). A common dream, often recurrent and indicative of conflictual anxiety about a subjectively perceived inescapable threat, which may suggest some early experiences of a similar nature embedded in Homer's mind and surfacing in his dreams.

60. "Truly a well-loved man do my eyes look on... and my heart is grieved for Hector who has burned for me many thighs of oxen..." Ibid., ll. 168 ff.

61. "A mortal man, doomed long since by fate, are you minded to free from dolorous death?" So does Athene challenge Zeus." Ibid., ll. 179 ff. "... then (Zeus) grasped the balance by the middle and raised it, and down sank the day of doom of Hector and went away to Hades; and Phoebus Apollo left him." Ibid., ll. 212-213.

62. Achilles tells to the dying Hector how "Pallas Athene vanquish you with my spear." (Ibid., l. 270).

63. Homer certainly did not lack in details when he described the similar duel between Hector and Aias Telamon: a duel without intervening gods and with an unclear outcome (*Iliad*, Book VII, ll. 246 ff.). As an aside, during the prolonged negotiations preceding that duel Agamemnon counsels his brother not to fight Hector because "even Achilles shudders to meet this man in battle . . . and he is far better than you." (Ibid. l. 113 ff.)

64. *Iliad*, Book XXII, ll. 346 ff.

65. She laments that Hector's body is "in the power of a violent man, in whose inmost liver I wish I could fix my teeth and feed on it" (*Iliad*, Book XXIV, ll. 211 ff.).

66. Consider variants of the statement "I love you so much that I could eat you whole."

67. And practically the only one; Achilles boasts on his exploits during the nine years of war, but this is his only actual appearance, in the *Iliad*, as a warrior. The point is interesting, in that he has prevalently been depicted as a quite inflated semi-divine figure, the prototype of the superhero.

68. If the twelve youths are discounted as not belonging to the slaying during combat, then Hector, with a total of twenty-nine enemies killed, has a higher score; and Diomedes, at twenty-two, is a close competitor.

69. *Iliad*, Book XVI, ll. 784-785.

70. *Iliad*, Book XXII, ll. 396 ff.

71. Ibid., l. 405. Achilles at this point could have continued to lead the victorious Achaean army and assault a city filled with defeated and leaderless soldiers and awash in grief: instead he decided to drag the body of Hector to the Greek camp, a trophy for Patroclus and a source of glory for himself.

72. Ibid., ll. 409 ff.

73. "... people were given over to wailing and groaning throughout the city. To this was it most like, as though all beetling Ilios were utterly burning with fire." (Ibid., ll. 408 ff.)

74. To his mother who came to try and console him he states: " but now let me win glorious renown and set many a one among the deep-bosomed Trojan and Dardanian women to wipe the tears from her tender cheeks with both hands and to moan ceaselessly." (Ibid. ll. 121 ff.). Hector was deeply hurt at having caused so much women's grief; Achilles is looking forward to cause it. The different level of empathy for feminine suffering—the connectedness with the inner anima—is remarkable.

75. It is interesting that these specific lines were rejected by Aristarchus.

76. But when noble Achilles had had his fill of weeping, and the desire of it had gone away from his heart and limbs, immediately then he sprang from his seat . . ." (Book XXIV, ll. 513 ff.)

77. Perhaps another one of those brilliant touches from Homer! Achilles had proffered a similar refusal to wash and eat until he could have what he wanted from the Achaeans: their immediate return into battle (Book XIX, ll. 200 ff.).

78. One has to wander whether Homer implies that Achilles is afraid of the wrath that Priam will feel should he witness how much abuse his son has suffered, and needs to clean the body up before presenting him to the father.

SIX
Concluding the Analysis on the Opening Demands

THE FIRST QUESTION REVISITED

The analysis of the material about the first question clarified the standing of the poet about Achilles and several Greek characters. He expresses consistently his position: the wrath of Achilles is unjustifiable on the official basis of dishonor; it is fierce, driven by an inflated search for revenge, ultimately truly accursed and "pitiless." He seems to imply that perhaps the true reason is lust for the absolute leadership and a burning urgency to depose, annihilate the father-master. Such a parricidal fantasy finds support in the hypothesis that something troublesome had happened during the period that the five-year-old Achilles spent at the court of Agamemnon, in the middle of that specific developmental phase categorized as oedipal by the Freudian system. In psychoanalytic theory, this is the stage in psychosexual development, known as the phallic phase, that usually occurs between the ages of three and seven, and is characterized by the manifestations of the Oedipus Complex: deep hostility toward fatherly figures, envy, jealousy, aggressive fantasies of getting rid of them and assuming their roles. The oedipal fantasy became activated, almost to its full realization, already in Book I, where it had been enhanced by the complete constellation of the oedipal triad (Achilles, Briseis, Agamemnon).[1] Homer seems to have been aware of this grandiose fantasy for exclusive alfa status and supreme leadership with elimination of the parental image, and provided it with further material in Book XXI, in which Achilles seems to stand in a fictional landscape, creating havoc among the enemy and being literally immersed in a river of blood.[2]

Conscious that he could not directly express to Greek audiences his prevalently negative opinion on Greek aggression and on the most exalted Greek hero who fought and died on the Ilian plain, Homer had it expressed by other highly revered Greek heroes, as Aias, Odysseus, and the great Patroclus, as well as by several gods as Zeus and Apollo. It is also noticeable, and telling, that nowhere in the *Iliad* could one find any heartfelt praise for the Pelides, except perhaps from Thetis: not even from old Phoenix, or from Patroclus himself.

Homer had also to be attentive in dealing with figures like Agamemnon, and any criticism had to be expressed though the statements of other great kings. I already reported the importance of this diplomatic approach earlier on, in my note on the Argives reactions to his poetry. By using this ruse, Homer was able to create veridical, rich and stable characters, and to convey his emotional ties to them. His Agamemnon was flawed but human, apparently overwhelmed at times by the complexity of his role, skeptical that he could actually pull it through and consequently very touchy about his honor, and fearful for his own life; therefore, he was prone to project upon other kings his fluctuating level of commitment, but also ready to seek their critical support and advice. For Aias Telamon the poet had unwavering respect and admiration, the peak of his emotional connectedness with this character appearing during the struggle of the Telamon on the bridge of Agesilaus' ship, and, later on, over the body of Patroclus. Similarly, Homer has favorable and frequent comments for Diomedes, who emerges in the *Iliad* as a most valiant and honorable warrior, a peer to Aias Telamon, whom he bests during the funeral games, and more feared than Achilles by the Trojans. The favorite of Athene, who even drove his chariot, he was the only human to be granted some permission to fight the gods; Homer acknowledged his wisdom on several occasions, and detailed his fighting experience and courage during his aristeia, the longest in the epic.

Sprouting probably from the telling and retelling since his Smyrna childhood, the mind of Homer was attracted by the legendary figures of Greek heroes as Patroclus, as Aias, as Diomedes, and even as old Nestor with his endless commentaries, and his son Antilochus. There is an emotional coloring accompanying these characters that indicates how their traits are ego-syntonic with Homer. Persistent qualities as honorable behavior and respect appear to be the common qualities in all of Homer's favorite characters, irrespective of the side in the war assigned to them by Fate.

Finally, Homer, as we have seen, accompanies his assessment and analysis of the major Greek actors with some critical considerations of the Achaean army, not failing to compare it to the Trojan forces.

The analysis can now move to the information about the poet's psychic inclination that emerges from his dealing with the second question and related themes.

THE SECOND QUESTION: HOMER AND THE DIVINE DIMENSION

Homer left no direct information about his personal religiosity, whether he worshipped the gods, and which ones. The entire epic, though, is redolent with the numinous element, and the poet provides a rich, almost constant divine fabric surrounding and enmeshed in human events. There is almost no scene in which the gods do not play multiple and often contrasting roles. Their assiduous presence confirms the description by Bryce reported earlier on, concerning their ubiquity in all aspects of human life. Homer clearly instills this feeling of an overarching divine dimension, a gestalt, or Fate, always in close proximity with the human one: a sort of divine firmament, out of which the individual gods descend at their leisure to act their personal deeds, or to respond to special calls, and then depart till the next unpredictable time and purpose. As I pointed out earlier, in Jungian psychological terms Fate represents the entire archetypal firmament, with its complex set of diverse organizing themes and motifs.

The gestalt is the implicit and explicit matrix of the human universe, a given for any audience, that does not require reminders. It is not so, instead, for the specific interventions of the deities, acting either individually or in concert with each other. These interventions need to be explained and understood, case by case, so that the audiences could have a grasp at any deeper meaning in the developmental dynamics of specific human events.

This would be the case for the few lines in Book XXIV concerning the judgment of Paris.[3] Homer travelled here beyond the Iliadic time window and showed his awareness of the dynamic antecedents to the Trojan tragedy, which were illustrated in the sagas of that period. The Cypria described the dynamics eventuating in the Trojan War. These started with the decision by Zeus to relieve through war the body of his mother Rhea, the Earth, burdened by too large a population.[4] The poem then described how Zeus and Themis orchestrated the events that would ultimately trigger that war, through the judgment of Paris.

It is important in the analysis of Homer's mind and of the *Iliad* to keep in the forefront the psychodynamic evolution of the conflict and its attached critical judgment. With those few lines near the end of the Epic Homer reminds the audience that humans were not actually responsible for the entire tragedy at Troy. Paris and Helen—and consequently the Trojans—had been forced into their roles by the inescapable powers of Zeus and Aphrodite.[5] Humans had been simply pawns in a tragic game that was preordained by Zeus and sustained by the jealous, implacable wrath of Hera and Athene, who, at the wedding of Thetis with Peleus, both coveted, together with Aphrodite, the golden apple that divine Discord, who had not been invited, had thrown among the goddesses as a prize for the "most beautiful of them all." To the barely adolescent (and sex hormones driven) Paris,[6] whom Zeus had chosen to decide who would be the winner, they had promised magnificent gifts as bribes: Hera offered to make him the king of Europe and Asia Minor, Athene offered him wisdom and skill in battle; but Aphrodite promised him the most beautiful woman on Earth, and won the context. The extent of the divine wrath, out of being deprived of a prize, with lack of recognition and with "dishonor"—Hera primarily, Athene more subdued to her father's will—finds its human expression in the similarly rooted wrath of Achilles. He becomes the tool for the goddesses to get their revenge.

Perhaps nowhere else as in the tragedy of Paris and Helen does the human role appear as solely a tool of divine organizing patterns. In Book III, the human Paris attempts to undo the Trojan fate by dueling with Menelaus: the winner will take Helen and the war will end. He loses, but the gods do not permit the human resolution: Aphrodite snitches Paris away from Menelaus' killing stroke and deposits him in the bed of unwilling but compelled Helen; then, Zeus and Athene make sure that the peace treaty is broken by compelling Pandarus to shoot an arrow and wound Menelaus, triggering Agamemnon's retaliation by renewed fighting. Trojans and Greeks had loudly praised the treaty and the peace; their fate and their wishes are insignificant in face of the opposite archetypal demands.

The analysis of the spiritual dimension of the poet, and of its organizing factors, needs not to be constrained by the fact that the *Iliad* appears to address exclusively Greek deities. The Greek and the Near Eastern religious cultures (including the western Anatolian seaboard kingdoms, the Hittites, and even the kingdom of Ugarit) shared a similar Pantheon of major gods, the difference often being only in the names. So, Greek Zeus, "the Clouds Gatherer" would identify with Hittite Tarhunt, "the Storm God" and with the Ugaritic gods Baal—the god of lightning, whose common poetic epithet was "Rider of the Clouds"—and his companion Hadad, god of storms and thunder. Baal' similarity to Zeus was also expressed by the belief—in the Baal cycle—that he had destroyed the god of Chaos, Yan, and created a new pantheon. These similarities between the two deities may have helped young Homer's mind to conglomerate them into a "two-faced" god. The Hittite counterpart of Aphrodite was Padritahi, that of Athene was Maliya; Apollo was mirrored in Iyarri; Ares in Astabis; and so on. The pantheons were then enriched by local deities, as the Trojan river gods Scamander and Simois. Therefore, while Homer appears to explicitly discuss Greek gods—for whatever reason: belief, political correctness, or personal safety!—he may in fact implicitly refer to their counterparts, under disguise.

Homer stressed the incessant involvement of the individual gods and he apparently enjoyed to capture, repeatedly and at length, their most evident personality traits, often all too human, and their interpersonal conflicts and alliances, while being careful to preserve the overall mantle of immortal powers able to act well above the human dimension. By the end of the Epic he put together rich and lively descriptions, and his implied preferences transpire, to the analyst, through the wordings used for each narrative.

His statements repeatedly endorse Zeus as the "king of all the Gods," and pay full respect to his great power, second only to Fate. Furthermore, Homer assigns to him a special affective proclivity for the Trojans, particularly for Priam and Hector, because of their impeccable devotion and equally impeccable offerings.[7] When Hector is gravely injured by a stone thrown to him by Aias, Zeus sends Apollo to heal and strengthen him.[8] The image of Zeus that transpires out of Homer's mind is a complex one, as the god navigates between his strong emotional response to the fates of Hector and of his own son Sarpedon, and his primary "planetary" goal of a decimating war, while dealing with all the idiosyncrasies and squabbles among the members of his pantheon and family. It is quite likely that during his spiritual development the poet, exposed to two different worlds, adapted conflicting information and ideologies by having Greek Zeus and Trojan Tarhunt coexist in the phase-space of his mental universe, as two simultaneous faces of the same divine reality.

By contrast, the most vivid and endearing representation of Hera is probably the one of her getting ready to seduce her husband.[9] The scene is a true gem in describing an aspect of Homer's mind somewhat detached from the war theme and also from religious constraints: in these lines[10] he reveals how in his fantasy he dresses, and undresses, a goddess, a muse, an ideal lover, responding to his personal and his societal value system on the issue, to include the choice of her hairdo and earrings; and he proceeds with the delightful, argute detail of Hera going to Aphrodite—the archrival who got the golden apple, the cause of the war and of the fierce jealousy among the goddesses—to ask for the bra "and (Aphrodite) loosed from her bosom the embroidered strap, inlaid, in which are fashioned all manner of allurement; in it is love, in it desire, in it dalliance-persuasion that steals the senses even of the wise"[11] in order to render her own breasts even more irresistible to Zeus. This is the same goddess who is frequently reproached by her husband as spiteful, devious, strange in her hatred, always complaining and seeking to cause trouble[12]; and repeatedly Homer describes her crafty lying; in Book XIV alone she straight-facedly lies to Aphrodite, to Zeus, and most likely to Sleep too, concerning the promise of the Grace Pasithea as a wedding gift.[13] She is even willing to sacrifice her three favorite cities in exchange for Troy![14]

This is not the case for Athene, the other main unrelenting enemy of the Trojans. She is probably the most significant and revered Greek goddess, born directly out of the head of Zeus, and Homer is quite attentive to point out her many interventions to help the Achaean army and the single kings, and her role in the duel and death of Hector. However, he is also aware from the past history that the goddess had been the guardian of the city, possibly as her local counterpart Maliya, and he does not fail to highlight this other relationship between Troy and Athene; her shrine, in the citadel, is the only shrine mentioned and described in the *Iliad*, inclusive of its priestess[15]; Hecabe goes there to pray the goddess for protection from Diomedes[16] and the priestess deposits a perfect robe as an offering on the knees of the Palladium. The Little Iliad[17] describes how Troy could not be taken as long as the wooden statue of Pallas Athene, the Palladium, was inside the city, and how eventually Odysseus, disguised as a beggar, would enter Troy and steal it. However, during the time span of the *Iliad*, the goddess was still in the complicated position of striving for a complete Trojan defeat and annihilation on the battlefield, while still protecting the city through her sacred simulacrum safely held inside the citadel! Once more, Homer appears to be working with double images; possibly the chosen path, in his mind, to recognize an intrinsically Near Eastern deity, and her Trojan saga, under the disguise of an overtly Greek one.

The role that Homer designs for Apollo is more straightforward; in addition to setting the stage for the confrontation between Achilles and Agamemnon, he is the protector of the city—when directed by Zeus, he carries the aegis for the Trojan army, and he stops Patroclus from scaling the wall—but primarily of Hector, alive as well as dead. He is also the advocate for the release of Hector's body, and he is the triggering voice for the condemnation by the gods of Achilles' impious behavior toward Hector. The god is the tool used by Homer to activate the two acts of Greek impiety that link the opening and the closing of the epic, through which the poet reveals, in a disguised fashion, his standing on the topic.

When considered in their entirety, the descriptions of Homer about the divine realm offer a significant perspective of his mental attitude toward the two systems of values that had confronted each other at Troy. In a sociocultural basin in which, I repeat it once more, the divine realm and its individual deities were an undisputed, and often even physical, reality, Homer ended up offering a sharp differentiation between Trojans and Mycenean Greeks on devotional attitude and reverence for the gods and their significance. During the course of coming into adulthood his experience in colonized Ionia and his acute ability in reading human characters had made him aware of Greece bellicose streak, its hubris, its investment in supremacy and in excelling upon men and even gods alike. He perceived, rightly, that the Greek audiences would have loved characters as Achilles and Diomedes; that they would have dismissed and antagonized any challenge to the supremacy of their pantheon; and that, by recognizing their own traits projected in their versions of the gods, they would have seen no wrong in the way the poet depicted some of the Olympians.

Of the four divine figures that I examined earlier on, the poet demonstrates respect and clear reverence for Zeus/Tarhunt, Athene/Maliya, and Apollo/Iyarri. I emphasize how all three deities belong to both Near Eastern and Western Pantheons and all of them are, or were, emotionally connected with Troy and its people as well as with Greece and her people (in two parallel, coexisting spiritual domains, so to speak).

Toward Hera, who perhaps was exclusively a Greek goddess—to my knowledge there was no correlate in the Anatolian pantheon—Homer, as described above, has a rather different attitude: she is a crafty, bitter, jealous liar, a critical and complaining spouse, forgivable because extremely appealing sexually, although her lovemaking is manipulative.[18] Her wrath against Troy (as mentioned she would sacrifice her three favorite cities in exchange for its destruction), because she felt dishonored and deprived of her prize, mirrors closely the wrath of Achilles.

The two-faced aspect of these deities in Homer's mind becomes quite apparent in the *Odyssey*, if indeed he had also composed this sequel to the *Iliad*. The poet vividly describes the second and wrath-filled face of Zeus and Athene, a face devastating to the Achaeans and many of their leaders, which emerged immediately after the fall of the city. The tragedy that befell on the kingdom of the Trojans and their allies finds its counterpoint (its revenge?) in the tragedy of the Achaean contingents and the dreadful fate spread by the gods on their victorious return to their motherlands. The army is scattered by repeated god-stirred strife between leaders and by powerful storms, despite useless attempts to propitiate the divine dimension through the offering of hecatombs. A great part of the army never reached their homes but died by drowning; others were driven by angry seas and fierce winds to distant lands, wandering for several years before being able to return decimated to their lands, many having been killed on the way home. The slaying of old Priam by young Neoptolemus, on the doorstep of his palace, is paralleled by the slaying of Agamemnon in his own palace, together with all his comrades, by Aegisthus, the lover of his wife Clytemnestra.[19]

To be on the safe side, Homer continues to express his different affective standing for the two opposing camps in his usual indirect way: he presents the other face of the two major deities, Zeus and Athene, through the words of Greek figures of renown. Thus, we hear Nestor telling Telemachus that "when we had sacked the lofty city of Priam . . . then Zeus planned in his heart a woeful return for the Argives, since by no means were all prudent and just"[20]; and again: "Zeus did not yet purpose our return, stubborn god, who roused evil strife again a second time."[21] He also describes "the terrible wrath of the flashing-eyed goddess . . . for she caused strife between the two sons of Atreus,"[22] and how "Agamemnon . . . wished . . . that he might appease the dread wrath of Athene—fool! . . . she was not to hearken."[23] Menelaus will describe to the son of Odysseus that "Aias Oileus was lost amid his long-oared ships ... would have escaped his doom, hated by Athene though he was, had he not uttered a boastful word in great blindness of heart."[24] And Odysseus, too, will share with the ghost of Aias Telamon that: "No other is to blame but Zeus, who bore terrible hatred against the army of the Danaan spearmen, and brought on you your doom."[25]

Homer packed the story of Odysseus' return to Ithaca with fantastic adventures and with narratives of what happened after Hector's death. One encounters the entire set of sagas that made the content of the Epic Cycle, and more: the poet mentions "the quarrel between Odysseus and Achilles, son of Peleus, how once they strove with violent words at a rich feast of the gods, and Agamemnon, king of men, was glad at heart that the best of the Achaeans were quarreling, for thus Phoebus Apollo, in giving his response, had told him that it should be, in sacred Pytho. . . . For then the beginning of woe was rolling upon Trojans and Danaans alike through the will of great Zeus."[26] S. Butler, in his translation of the epics (p. 498), states that "no account of this quarrel by any Greek poet has come down to us." It sounds very unlikely, if not truly impossible, that a highly skilled minstrel as Homer would invent ex novo an anecdote of such apparent magnitude to the unfolding of the Trojan war without enriching it for the audiences into a more elaborate version. This would not have reflected Homer's style; after all, he was alluding to an intriguing strife between two major heroes at a divine feast, an equally intriguing secret pleasure of Agamemnon as he witnessed the strife, an arcane consultation of the Delphic oracle and Apollo's predictions of great woes for Danaans and Trojans alike. It seems that the poet referred to an episode that he took for granted would be well known to his contemporary audiences. Unfortunately, the episode and its attached saga faded into obscurity by the time Greece entered into its Classical period. If it had appeared anywhere in the Epic Cycle it did not survive in any of the fragments and in the subsequent summaries; perhaps it had been part of the work that Proclus implies had preceded the Cypria and that apparently described the divine unfolding of the Trojan tragedy.

If all this material from different sources were to be accepted in the psychodynamic analysis of Homer's Iliadic mind, it would reinforce the theme of the affective divine preference for the Trojans that Homer, as we demonstrated, infused in his *Iliad*; and the faces of Anatolian Tarhunt and Maliya would assume a clearer definition as the opposite sides of those belonging to Greek Zeus and Athene.[27]

The analyst needs to activate her or his skill for intersubjective understanding and to keep in mind how much the child growing up in Smyrna, or Chios, had already perceived the religious dimension as an essential aspect of life, while being surrounded by divine presences coming in different versions, the Mycenean-Greek and the Trojan-Anatolian. By the time this material coalesced into the *Iliad*, Homer had developed a different emotional reaction to the two different levels of devotion and piety observable among the Greeks and the Trojans, and showed greater connectedness with the Trojan version. This conclusion is based on several findings—emerging from the analysis of the Iliadic religious themes and statements—that trace a visible pattern of the "motus cordis" of the poet. The most significant are summarized below.

Homer failed to describe any instance of Trojan impiety that would balance the lack of reverence and the disregard for divine dictates and expectations shown in Book I by Agamemnon and by Achilles in Books XXIII and XXIV. He did describe in details the defiance of the sacred oath pledged before the duel between Menelaus and Paris, but, as I already mentioned, he put great emphasis in placing the responsibility of its transgression fully on the shoulders of (δαιμονίη) Hera, Zeus, and Athene,[28] who persuaded the archer Pandaros, a Trojan ally, "to let fly a swift arrow at Menelaus," by promising great gifts and honor, and the protection of Apollo.

He reported the repeated statements by Zeus praising the high degree of reverence and devotion professed by Priam and Hector, but left a glaring omission of divine praise for similar examples out of the Greek camp.

Finally, he called Ilium "holy" at least two dozen times. If the sociocultural basin of his mind had been prevalently a Greek one, there would have been no place for such a significant tribute to the royal center of the hatred Trojans, the symbol of their culture, which the Greeks wanted to destroy at all costs. The persistent emergence of this Greek-dystonic symptom strongly suggests the presence of a strong Trojan-syntonic attractor imbedded in the phase-space of his mind and imposing a specific directional weight to the psychodynamic process.

The analysis just concluded of the two questions that provide the putative themes directing the entire Epic has given a robust evidence that the *Iliad*, in Homer's mind, is not necessarily a glorification of the semi-divine figure of Achilles, nor of Greek might. Furthermore, while Homer shows true admiration for several Greek heroes, the assessment of his vision of the divine dimension strongly suggests that his movement of the heart was a Trojan one.

A complete analysis of the *Iliad* demands therefore that some consideration be given also to the Trojan aspect: to the mental images of Homer as he transports himself inside the walls of Troy; and how they are transmitted into his work.

NOTES

1. Prof. Cabaniss defines this triad as the "three-persons relationship": the child, the opposite sex love object, the same sex rival. (*Psychodynamic Formulation*, p. 102).

2. The scene brings to mind the description of Ramesses II at Kadesh, when he fought alone and put to flight 2,500 Hittite chariots, "sprawling before my horse"

(Kadesh Inscription after Gardiner, reported in Bryce, *The Kingdom of the Hittites*, p. 238).

3. "they [Hera and Athene] . . . became hateful . . . because of the folly of Alexander, who had insulted those goddesses when they came to his farmstead and praised her who furthered his grievous lustfulness." (Book XXIV, ll. 27 ff.)

4. "in his wise heart resolved to relieve the all-nurturing earth of men by causing the great struggle of the Ilian war, that the load of death might empty the world. And so the heroes were slain in Troy, and the plan of Zeus came to pass." (Schol. On Homer, Il. i. 5 #3, LCL #57, p. 497).

5. Priam mentions this point when he kindly tells Helen "you are in no way to blame in my eyes; it is the gods, surely, who are to blame, who roused against me the tearful war of the Achaeans." (*Iliad*, Book III, ll. 164 ff.)

6. At this point in the saga Paris, alias Alexander, was as yet an unknown son of Priam, who had been cast away to the wild beasts at birth by his mother Hecabe, scared by a dreadful dream, and had been rescued and raised by shepherds as their own son.

7. "For of all the cities beneath the sun and starry heaven in which men reared on the earth have their abodes, of these sacred Ilios was most honored in my heart, and Priam, and the people of Priam of the good ashen spear. For never at any time was my altar lacking in the equal banquet, the drinks offering, and the savor of burnt offering, for that is the privilege we gods have received." *Iliad*, Book IV, ll. 44 ff. "Truly a well-loved man do my eyes look on . . . and my heart is grieved for Hector, who has burned for me so many thighs of oxen on the crests of many-ridged Ida, and at other times on the topmost citadel." (*Iliad*, Book XXII, ll. 168 ff.)

8. *Iliad*, Book XV, ll. 231 ff.

9. It is also much more successful than the preceding one, when she got elaborately ready for war, together with Athene, only to be quickly deflated by Zeus' threat of serious punishment. This time she dropped the manly role, shifted to the feminine alluring one, and got what she wanted.

10. *Iliad*, Book XIV, ll. 169 ff.

11. Ibid., ll. 214 ff.

12. ". . . she angers me with taunting words . . . she constantly reproaches me . . ." (*Iliad* Book I , ll. 519 ff.); "You are incredible (δαιμονίη)! You are for ever imagining . . ." (Ibid., ll. 561 ff.); "Strange (δαιμονίη) queen, in what way do Priam and the sons of Priam work you so many ills that you rage incessantly to lay waste. . . . Ilios?" *Iliad* Book IV, ll. 31 ff.); "she is always in the habit of thwarting me in whatever I have decreed." (*Iliad*, Book VIII, ll. 408 ff.). By having Zeus address his wife at times with the vocative δαιμονίη—a daimon—Homer describes her as being directed by and representing an ill-omened, malignant divine power.

13. *Iliad*, Book XIV, ll. 267 ff.

14. She tells Zeus, who questions her request that Troy be destroyed: "I have three cities that are far dearest in my sight, Argos and Sparta and broad-wayed Mycenae; lay these waste whenever they are hateful to your heart. Not in their defense do I stand before them, nor grudge you in any way." (*Iliad*, Book IV, ll. 51 ff.)

15. *Iliad* Book VI, ll.

16. "Lady Athene, you who guard our city, fairest among goddesses, break now the spear of Diomedes . . . but Pallas Athene denied the prayer." Ibid., ll. 297 ff

17. LCL # 57, p. 509.

18. In her defense, one may want to recall her words to Thetis: "you did not deign to lie down in the bed of Zeus when he desired it for he is always preoccupied with these acts, whether sleeping with immortals or with mortal women"! (*Argonautica*, Book IV, ll. 793 ff.)

19. Aeschylus in his Agamemnon tragedy offers a different ending to the life of the Atreides. His wife will kill him in revenge for the sacrifice of Iphigenia, and will also kill Cassandra, who had been raped at Troy by Aias Oileus on the altar of Athene/

Maliya—the likely cause for the goddess' rage at him—and then taken as slave and concubine by Agamemnon.

20. *Odyssey*, Book III, ll. 131 ff.
21. Ibid., ll. 160 ff.
22. Ibid., ll. 135 ff.
23. Ibid., ll. 143 ff. A counterpoint (balancing act?) to her denying the prayer of her Trojan priestess lady Theano, in the *Iliad*, (Book VI, l. 311).
24. *Odyssey*, Book IV, ll. 499 ff.
25. *Odyssey*, Book XI, ll. 559 ff.
26. *Odyssey*, Book VIII, ll. 75 ff.
27. Or perhaps it would reveal that the Achaeans were not immune from the grand plan of Zeus to decimate the human race; they had been the tool for the first slaughter on the Ilean fields; they now became the slaughtered ones.
28. "The father of men . . . immediately spoke to Athene . . . try to arrange it that the Trojans are first in defiance of their oath to work evil on the triumphant Achaeans." (*Iliad*, Book IV, ll. 68 ff.)

SEVEN
Homer and the Trojans

GLIMPSES IN THE CITY

The available material about Homer describing Trojan characters and attitudes is significantly limited in comparison with the abundance of data on the Greeks. It is sufficient, though, to present the reader with some significant vignettes of the life inside Troy during those fifty-one days; furthermore Homer, with his usual masterly skill in the choice of words, suggested revealing comparisons between the Greek and the Trojan handling of similar situations.

The poet introduces the figures of Priam and Helen in Book III. The Spartan princess is informed by Iris that Menelaus and Paris will confront each other for her sake and to end the war. She goes to the Scaean Gate, where "the elders of the people" are sitting on the wall along with Priam. They are described as "good speakers, like cicadas," a likely equivalent to old Nestor, but Homer, capturing with just a few lines their garrulous chatting and their whispering to each other how Helen is stunningly alluring, adorable, and yet the Trojans need to get rid of her,[1] makes them more real in their humanity and "lily-like" voices than the long-winded and somber, pontificating Nestor, who seems never able to give advice without first recounting his own heroic actions under similar circumstances in the past. Priam promptly counteracts the softly spoken "winged words" of his counselors: he calls Helen: "come here dear child, and sit in front of me . . . you are in no way to blame in my eyes; it is the gods, surely, who are to blame, who roused against me the tearful war." Homer will, later on, contrast these gentle and caring words of the old king with those of Achilles describing Helen as "abhorred" one.[2]

Homer returns to the city in Book VI, one of the most emotionally evocative, and rich in plain humanity. While in the midst of battle, Hector is directed by his brother Helenus "far the best of diviners," to go back to Ilios and urge their mother to gather the older women at the shrine of Athene and propitiate the goddess with proper prayers and bountiful offerings "to have compassion on the city and the Trojans' wives and their little ones."[3]

At the Scaean gate Homer portrays Hector being surrounded by distressed women running to him for news about "their sons and brothers and friends and husbands" and counseling them, in turns, to raise prayers to the gods; the poet adding that "over many were sorrows hung."[4]

After having conveyed to his mother the directives from Helenus, and shown to her his instinctive respect on how to properly address the gods—certainly not while one is "all befouled with blood and filth"—Hector goes first to the living quarters of Helen and Paris. His last words to his mother—and they will be, indeed, the last words he would ever speak to her—carry very clearly what the entire city feels about his brother: "I will go after Paris . . . I wish that the earth would gap for him at once! For the Olympian has reared him as a great bane to the Trojans and great-hearted Priam, and to the sons of Priam. If I should see him going down to the house of Hades, then I would say that my heart had forgotten its grief."[5] Once more, Homer reiterates how the bane on Troy was "reared" by Zeus, the Olympian, and not by intrinsic human behavior. By having Hector address his brother as δαιμόνι', the poet emphasizes the "daimon" that has taken possession of Paris; and he uses the dialogue between Hector and Helen to reinforce this message and to hint at future events, and their possible link.

Helen tells Hector that "on us Zeus has brought an evil doom, so that even in days to come we may be song for men that are yet to be"; and Hector responds that he wants to go and see his wife and child "for I know not if any more I shall return to them again, or if even now the gods will vanquish me at the hands of the Achaeans."

Everything that Homer presents has a precise meaning, in his mind, and a precise place in the sequence, even if restrained by the templates of epic poetry and the requirements for metrical correctness (and the politics of Greece!). Three times by now, in fairly close sequence, the poet clears the Trojans, as well as Paris and Helen, from any responsibility in the tragedy played out at Troy, and deposits the blame at the feet of the gods, Zeus and Hera primarily: a rather persuasive exoneration that reframes the ethical landscape and the standing of the players.

Then he introduces the idea of a song for future generations; a song for Helen and Paris as individuals, but also, inevitably, for all those entrapped with them by the scheming of Zeus. Such a prediction by a character as Helen sounds rather suspiciously as a reference to the *Iliad* (and, perhaps, to the sagas of the Epic Cycle dealing with the fate of the city). What was in Homer's mind when he put those words in her mouth?

He knew that his work was about the bane of Troy; the story of Paris and Helen tragedy; but also, in a brilliant connection, he linked the song of Helen to the prediction of Hector concerning his impending death mandated by the gods. His song, Homer seems to imply, is about the tragedy of Troy and that of his sole protector: a few lines later, Homer will state that "only Hector guarded Ilios."

What follows has been widely recognized as possibly the most tender and human vignette of the entire *Iliad*. Hector rushes across the city to the Scaean Gate, looking for his wife, and there she comes running to him, followed by a maid carrying their son, "a mere baby, well-loved ... like a fair star." They speak to each other at length, both aware of the impending doom. Andromache, weeping and clasping her husband's hands, implores him to spare himself, to fight from within the protection of the walls; she feels the upcoming tragedy and begs him to have pity for his family: if he leaves the safety of the city she "will soon be your widow ... never will any comfort be mine, when you have met your fate, but only woes"; and he will make his son fatherless.[6] Andromache uses the vocative term δαιμονίη to address her husband, as being possessed and driven by his bravery, perceived as a dark side within, a daimon that will destroy him.

Hector shares with her that he has the same worries and that "I know this well in my mind and heart: the day will come when sacred Ilios will fall, and Priam, and the people of Priam"; and he is already deeply troubled by "your grief, when some bronze-clad Achaean will lead you away weeping and rob you of your day of freedom."[7] Still, how could he face the Trojans, and their wives, if he did not join his army fighting down in the plain, and sought cowardly refuge behind the walls of the city?

Hector then turns his attention to his son and Homer not only portrays beautifully the immediate lifting of the parents' mood as they witness the child's reaction to his father's "bronze and the crest of horsehair ... waving terribly from the top of the helmet", and share with each other a brief moment of joy[8]; the poet also perceives the sudden fear in the mind of the child, and his reaction; and then, quite accurately, the soothing and loving response of the father. The encounter ends when Hector "placed his child in his dear wife's arms, and she took him to her fragrant bosom, smiling through her tears, and her husband was touched with pity at the sight of her, and he stroked her with his hand, and spoke to her, and called her by name."[9]

Across the river, one hundred thousand men—sons, brothers, husbands—symbolize and carry in themselves broken families in deep anguish. It should be a rich ground for similar personal expressions of human distress, reminiscences of a particular emotionally meaningful bonding, or genuine signs of caring, like a touch or a gentle word. Instead Homer is overall silent, apart from Briseis—a Trojan captive!—toward Patroclus; and, shortly after that, Achilles, while still weeping for Patroclus, recalls his own father—he will long for him again, the memories stirred by Priam, in Book XXIV—and, very briefly, his son Neoptolemus; "so he spoke weeping, and to it the elders added their laments, remembering each one what he had left at home."[10] Homer's empathy for the Greeks facing death, loss and separation is present, but what are missing are specific Greek memories and manifestations of interpersonal tenderness and love. The difference between the behavior of Achilles toward Briseis, compared to that of Hector toward Andromache, is a loud indicator of Homer's movement of the heart. The affect-rich image of an Achilles who found a word and a brief caress for his distressed "wife," when she was taken away from him by the heralds, would have provided, already in Book I, a powerful and balancing contrast to the strife-driven figure of Pelides!

BOOK XXIV: A DESCRIPTIVE ANALYSIS

Every work of literary art, be it a piece of writing, a play, a tragedy (as well as every psychotherapeutic journey), is structured with a beginning in which the presenting complaint, psychic complex, main thematic motifs, are already present, even if hidden from sight; then the long path of elaboration and development follows; and finally the process reaches its conclusion, its "raison d'être," and its sense of closure. The creator tends then to orchestrate a description, a scene, that captures that conclusion and encapsulates the main reason for the entire project and its journey.

Homer's concluding chapter (Book XXIV) is about grief.

It starts with the grief and rage of Achilles and it presents immediately the gruesome, highly disturbing vision of dead Hector dragged thrice, each day at dawn, around the mound of Patroclus; and then being left there, "outstretched on his face in the dust." The goal of Achilles is indeed Hector's defacement, which is undone daily by Apollo with his golden aegis,[11] until the majority of the gods becomes disgusted, and Zeus orders to Achilles through his mother to desist and give the body of Hector back because "Hector too was dearest to the gods of all mortals that are in Ilios" and "I above all immortals am filled with wrath."

Homer's intuitive ability for deep empathic assessments of the human spirit seems to surface once more in these few lines in which the poet appears to masterly capture what often is a crucial struggle in the therapeutic journey: the Ego's attempt to erase by defensive maneuvers the disturbing symbols and the discordant pressure from the true self; or from the personal shadow; or the "other within." In the case of Achilles it was the specular and opposite hero image with his reversed roles represented by Hector: a fully human family man (not solely a briefly mentioned son and an unmentioned wife or seduced maiden[12]); a protector rather than a destroyer; a figure acting out of care and sorrow (a bit like

Patroclus), rather than guilt and rage. In the reality of Homer's mind and of depth psychology these attempts, to secure one's existence as a reconstructed self-vision anchored in the present—and separated from the past by defensive denial, paranoid aggressive devaluation, and dismemberment of past memories and experiences—cannot ultimately succeed. Hector's symbolism is rooted in—and protected by—the archetypal domain, the "spirit of the depth": templates of eternal significance, largely immune from the variables of time.)

With this set of opening images Homer reconnects the audience with the similar scene seen from the walls of Troy in Book XXII, and with the deep despair of the parents and wife, as well as the loud grieving of the entire population, as they see their son, husband, greatest hero and protector of all, being dragged in such ignominious way, his face being lacerated and disfigured beyond recognition. Having reestablished the affective link, the poet continues the narrative from where he had left it off in order to follow Achilles; Priam, his head and neck covered by "filth in abundance which he had gathered in his hands as he groveled on the earth,"[13] is now "close-wrapped" in his mantle[14] and sits on the floor of his court surrounded by his remaining sons who drench their clothing with tears, while the house is filled with the wailing of women lamenting their many losses.

The old king's anguish for Hector's death and, possibly even more, for the despoiling and the lack of a proper funeral, continues in his bitter rebuke at the remaining sons: he recalls the best ones he lost, while "these things of shame are all that remains, liars and dancers."

Grief and anger do not distract him from giving careful devotional attention and not letting the dirt that covers him contaminate his prayer to Zeus,[15] requested by Hecabe, for a safe journey and a true messenger, after he receives the divine directive to go to the Greek camp and to Achilles. Grief and anger, in different manifestations, will color the entire encounter with Achilles; before that, though, Homer draws the image of the two old men, Priam and the herald, halting at the ford of the Scamander for the animals to drink, while "darkness had by now come down over the earth," and with the fearful knowledge of the Achaeans "hostile men and shameless who are nearby." It is a poignant image; Homer underscores the dimension of the grief, expressed through love and bravery, driving Priam forward; and it connects with that of Chryse walking in daylight into the Greek camp for another ransom.

The extent of the king's abnegation for the sake of Hector is also captured by the words he uses to mollify Achilles: "I have endured what no other mortal on the face of earth has yet endured, to reach out my hand to the face of the man who has slain my sons."

As already mentioned, Achilles joins Priam in grieving, but briefly: the king's grief, instead, is enduring, and it fosters his demands to be allowed to look at the body of Hector, with the dire, threatening consequences described earlier. However, once Achilles has been able to hide from Priam the view of Hector stretched out in the dirt, and has the body washed, draped in white linens, and loaded on the cart, some of his brusque and arrogant mood changes. He still does not allow the king to have a look at his son until morning, but assures him that he will restrain the Achaean army for as long as needed to provide for a proper funeral.

Then the theme pervading this last chapter moves back to Troy. Priam and the herald slipped away from the hut of Achilles and the camp of the Achaeans, with the help of Hermes. As they, wailing and moaning, got close to the city and dawn started to spread her saffron robe over the earth, the entire population of Troy, alerted by Priam's daughter Cassandra, poured out of the Scaean gate, "for on all came unbearable grief, and hard by the gates they met Priam . . . and the people thronged about and wept. And now the whole day long . . . would they have made lament for Hector with shedding of tears there outside the gates, if the old man had not spoken"make way for the mules to pass through; then shall you take your fill of wailing, when I have brought him into the house."[16] In a somber, sadness-filled way Homer spends the rest of his *Iliad* to describe the grief of the city, interspersed with melancholic songs and with lamentations and premonitions of doom, among which those of Hecabe and Helen, and Andromache's heart-breaking prediction of her son being hurled from the wall, "a woeful death." For nine days the city lamented while preparing the pyre, and on the tenth day "they carried bold Hector out, shedding tears, and on the topmost pyre they laid the dead man and cast fire on it."[17] On the following day they collected the bones in a golden urn, placed it in a hollow grave covered with great stones, and raised a mound over it before returning for "a glorious feast in the halls of Priam." The *Iliad* then closes with one last line: "in this way they held funeral for horse-taming Hector."

BOOK XXIV: A PSYCHOLOGICAL ASSESSMENT

What could Homer signify, by choosing this ending to his creation?

By now, the analysis of his available developmental history, including the myth-shrouded data about his childhood, and his chronological location in relation to the Trojan war, suggested a mental phase-space in which the Greek theme was historically inevitable, but possibly emotionally limited and conflicted. Most of the data suggest a prevalence of—and identification with—the local history and the impact of the old war on the spirit of the region.

Before proceeding further, it is essential to bring back in the foreground the political situation for the lands colonized by Greece and the extent, drive, and harshness of Greek imperialistic expansionism. Once more, one has to recall its pattern spanning from the complaints of Hittite emperors to a Mycenean king—possibly Atreus—to the political decision of the enlightened, post Solon Athenians concerning Samos resistance to their requests; and expressed repeatedly and clearly by Homer in the many Greek plans to plunder and destroy the city, slaughter all the Trojans and allies, and enslave their women.

The analysis of the first demand—the theme of Achilles—has clarified that Homer's attitude toward him was overall a negative one. It would be the topic of an entire new psychological work to try and identify the reasons for Pelides' everlasting glory in the western sociocultural basin,[18] but such image—the one I also shared, perhaps blinding myself to the affective incongruities in the Homeric text[19]—does not survive a critical analysis, and therefore this overtly Greek theme was not a primary stimulus to the Poet's work. It offered, though, a scaffold to the Greek epic and a needed crucial element to the Trojan tragedy.[20]

When one abandons Achilles as the real "muse," the inspirational factor of the *Iliad*—in therapy one would eventually abandon a phenomenological focus in search for the underlying psychic determinant system—and follows the current of emotions rather than the current of actions, then the epic of military might and individual prowess with arms on the battlefield becomes transformed into a tragedy of undeserved fate and harsh historical necessity.

The "Trojan tragedy" starts in Book I, with the impious abuse of a Trojan priest by the leader of the invading forces. Although Apollo tries to even the score, him being the only consistently pro-Trojan god, the consequences of his intervention are seriously counterproductive: they simply arm the bomb that will detonate in Book XXII.

By Book VI, the tragedy theme is well established: the gods do not allow the war to end, although all the Trojans as well as the Achaeans would, without hesitation. Therefore, the theme of grief starts to emerge: subtly, it did in the words of Priam to Helen in Book IV; then, clearly, during the encounter between Andromache and her husband—the last time they will talk, and share feelings, and touch each other.

But it is only starting with Book XXII, after the death of Hector, that the *Iliad* becomes primarily a poem about collective grief: mostly the grief of the city, but Homer, as is his fashion, also presents his audiences with the two very diverse expressions of grief: the Greeks grieving Patroclus and Trojans grieving Hector.

Homer fills the funeral of Patroclus with deeply dark images: the troubled ghostly appearances of the deceased, the hideous slaughtering of sacrificial animals and humans on the pyre, and the failure of the blood-soaked wood to ignite naturally, without a divine intervention; he then concludes it with the funeral games: a series of competitions among the most skilled warriors, which runs for almost the entire book.[21]

When one puts side by side Homer's descriptions of the expression of grieving from the entire population of the Greek camp and that from the population of Troy, both lamenting about the loss of one man, the difference is significant, even if the meaning of the difference may be obscure.

In the Greek camp grief is expressed, in a pathological way, primarily by a single person, after an initial period of interference due to Achilles' narcissistic disregard of the love object's need for a burial, and his obsession with personal revenge. It is then celebrated with multiple sacrificial victims and with the participation of all the Achaeans; and it culminates, in a formulaic fashion, with a prolonged demonstration of martial arts during which Patroclus is actually never mentioned and the general mood—including the one of Achilles—reflects the games and not their occasion. Then grief continues as rage and obsessive projective punishment of a corpse.

In the Trojan camp grief starts as a shared and intense experience in Book XXII, magnified in the desperate and deeply touching image of Hecabe offering to her son her old naked breast, the ultimate motherly love offering. It continues in Book XXIV, as the profound lament of an entire people grieving their city and their own existence as well as their hero, accompanied by the melancholy of the sung dirge; it forms the background to the gradual building of the pyre and its burning to ashes; to the burial of Hector's bones; and to the glorious banquet in the royal house.

The comparison highlights the unspoken closing Iliadic message that Homer is deeply grieving the tragedy of the kingdom of Priam and its alliance, and of its foremost hero and symbol. This seems to be the real motif of the *Iliad*: a eulogy to the culture and disappearance of his motherland. By putting together a saga that deeply stirred the pride and the attention of Greece, and by entrusting the colonial power with its praise and its dissemination, he assured that the memory of Troy, of that war and of the tragic fate of its heroes, would survive in a way that none of the Achaean centers of that period ever would: not a Mycenae, not Argos, not Sparta.[22]

The poem is, undeniably, about that clash of two civilizations and cultures, and the doomed efforts of Hector and a few others to stave off a defeat that they knew was inevitable: the forces were too unbalanced, and the Greeks were too hungry for the region's lands and riches. The theme of Trojan grief finally emerges to close the epic and to convey its true meaning. Homer has accomplished his vision: he has given appropriate—and sincere—consideration to Greek military power and resilience; has genuinely praised several of her greatest heroes, as Aias, Diomedes, Patroclus; has subtly but programmatically looked into the opening questions in order to illustrate his critical impression about Greek piety and about the wrath of Achilles, while maintaining for the Greek audiences this spurious but highly effective hero figure, a name that, linked to Troy, will assure its everlasting fame; now he can join the people of Troy in their somber funeral of the protector of the city, a function lapidary in its emotional intensity; and conclude the *Iliad* with the last, all-capturing verse: "in this way they held funeral for horse-taming Hector."

It is my hope that the collected documentation has illustrated in a sufficient manner the deeper level at which the mind of Homer operated to express and honor the tragedy of his putative motherland and her heroes under the screen of a paean for Greece's might. The affective tapestry of the epic is infiltrated with the awareness of the city's impending doom and with pervasive grief. Homer's focus on those fifty-one days of summer was his reconstruction of the progression of all the elements—human and divine—that culminated with the death of Hector; and a eulogy to the end of all that he represented for the region.

In the last line of the *Iliad* the Trojans and their allies bury their independence, their culture, their gods.

Homer has nothing else to say; his tragedy is now completed.

In a personal note Dr. A. Bedi labeled the *Iliad* as a Trojan Horse. The comparison fits rather well, indeed. Within the visible exterior representing Greek might and power is hidden the true message of the epic: an attestation for generations to come of the long history and of the religious and sociocultural traditions of Priam's kingdom; a deep lamentation for its fate; and, through its grieving, a process of personal and social healing and renewal.[23]

NOTES

1. "Small blame that Trojans and well-greaved Achaeans should for such a woman long suffer woes; she is dreadfully like immortal goddesses to look on. But even so, though she is like them, let her go home on the ships, and not be left here to be a bane to us and to our children after us." (*Iliad*, Book III, ll. 158 ff.)
2. "For the sake of abhorred Helen I am warring with the men of Troy." (*Iliad*, Book XIX, l. 325).
3. *Iliad*, Book VI, ll. 95 ff. Homer repeatedly expresses his concern for the fate of Trojan children.
4. Ibid., l. 241.
5. Ibid., ll. 280 ff.
6. Book VI ll. 407 ff.
7. *Iliad*, Book VI, ll.444 ff.
8. "Aloud then laughed his dear father and queenly mother." (Ibid., l. 471).
9. Ibid., ll. 482 ff.
10. *Iliad*, Book XIX, ll. 338 ff.
11. "But Apollo kept all defacement from his flesh, pitying the warrior even in death, and with the golden aegis he covered him fully so that Achilles might not tear his body as he dragged him." (*Iliad*, Book XXIV, ll. 18 ff.)
12. Pseudo Apollodorus in his Bibliotheca (3.13.8) reports that adolescent Achilles, just before leaving for the first Trojan expedition, had a son from Deidameia, the daughter of king Lycomedes at whose Court in Scyros Thetis had hidden her nine year old son. The Cypria (LCL #17, p. 493) describes how Achilles, while returning from the first expedition, is forced by a storm to land in Scyros and marries Deidameia.
13. *Iliad*, Book XXIV, ll. 162 ff.

14. Almost ten centuries later a Caesar, deeply wounded by the acute grief from his adopted son's patricidal betrayal more than by the knives, would cover himself with his mantle —the toga—and give in to resigned acceptance of the psychic loss.

15. Homer connects the father with the son (Book VI) by the same devotional respect.

16. *Iliad*, Book XXIV, ll. 707 ff.

17. Ibid., ll. 785 ff.

18. Thetis would greatly appreciate this form of immortality achieved by her son.

19. What did a partial identification with the invincible and stunningly beautiful Achilles provide to an insecure young adolescent, as I was, subject to a complex emotional and physical reorganization out of the ongoing hormonal storm?

20. The Pindaric view of Achilles as a paradigm of intrinsic excellence (the view shared also by present-day Dr. Alexander) was not always consistent through the succeeding sociocultural systems, as Dr. K.C. King illustrates in her very detailed book on the figure of Pelides. A dark, and even brutal, rendition appeared in the works of Euripides and of the Roman poet Catullus, among others; overall, the symbolic significance of this heroic figure tended to reflect, and be adapted to, the prevailing value systems of each succeeding Zeitgeist.

21. Homer inserts here the argute episode of Antilochus' race, mentioned earlier on, by which he shows that Achilles would not hesitate to take well-earned prizes away, if he felt like. The poet did not need a second strife, but just to bring a point across, in yet another instance of his use of distant events linked by a similar affective message.

22. As mentioned already, around the end of the second millennium BC many Bronze Age cities underwent violent destruction, often by fire, for poorly understood reasons. In the diplomatic writings of that period a "sea people" was mentioned repeatedly as the culprit.

23. History informs us that Priam's brother Anchises and his son Aeneas, cousin of Hector, led the Dardanians in flight from burning Troy. They will eventually land in Italy, where they will be known as the Trojans, fulfilling the prophecy of Poseidon: "and now surely will the mighty Aeneas be king among the Trojans, and his sons' sons who will be born in days to come" (*Iliad*, Book XX, ll. 307 ff.). While Homer could not envision a Trojan Rome rising out of the flames of Troy, as the power that would conquer Greece, he did envision a new Trojan kingdom still ruled by Trojan kings from the same House of Laomedon, to which Priam belonged.

EIGHT
Homer and the Orient
Integrating Psychodynamics and History

The uncovering of a Trojan epic, with a well-developed Trojan motif as the analogical affective narrative, running sub rosa alongside the descriptive, cognitive Greek narrative, represented an unpredicted outcome of the psychodynamic analysis. The genetic and developmental factors in Homer's life that gave definition to the Trojan epic, consisting in Homer's birth dynamics and geographical location, and in the specific collective zeitgeist surrounding his early development, find further independent support and concordance from other historical sources that examined possible links between the Anatolian lore and the works of Homer.

In her essay "Homer and the Near East," Prof. S. Morris[1] covers several areas showing Oriental commonalities with the Homeric works. Her input as a classicist archeologist provides a different and valuable dimension to the phase-space out of which the figure of Homer emerged. In this concluding chapter I will rely on the material of her essay liberally and even verbatim.

She opens the essay with a compelling statement: "the poems of Homer and the Epic Cycle belong to the eastern Mediterranean; they share narrative elements with neighboring cultures since the Bronze Age, and show specific connection to Near Eastern history and mythology."[2] However, the divorce of science from the family of the arts and from religion that characterized the Illuminism, created a schism between Greece and the Near East, compounded by the political and ideological western attitudes toward the Orient.

In Prof. Morris' words, "Near Eastern influence on Homeric poetry only emerged fully after the Second World War," when the literary works from the Near East, Ugarit, and Hattusa became easily available to scholars.[3]

It is in the Sumerian and Akkadian libraries of Mesopotamia, and particularly in those from Ugarit in the Levant that one finds poems with a close connection to Homer; as the already mentioned epic of Gilgamesh, which shares with the *Odyssey*, as well as the *Iliad*,[4] several of its major themes, like those of the warrior-hero, a dangerous journey, interactions with gods and search for immortality,

The Gilgamesh Epic, between 1300 and 3000 BC, was elaborated out of the Atrahasis, an Akkadian poem with interesting similarities to the *Iliad* in the themes of the supreme god being distraught by the overpopulation and deciding to bring destruction to humanity by famine and by a major flood. The flood reminds the one described in the *Iliad* by the simultaneous action of the Scamander and the Simois: lines 3–9 of tablet III of the Sumerian version mention the words "river" and "riverbank," a likely allusion to a fluvial inundation by the Euphrates River, where the kingdom of Atrahasis was presumably located.

Among the primary sources of Oriental influence over the Homeric work Morris notes also how historical and ritual Hittite texts reveal patterns shared with Homer, especially in oaths, oracles, and mortuary rites. Many traditions resemble Greek poetry in their common Near Eastern (or Anatolian) sources, not inherited Indo-European patterns, and she recalls the similarity of military models in the fourteen-century annals of the Hittite emperor Mursili II to the encounter of Achilles and Aeneas reported earlier.

While researching the historical connections and conditions, Morris examines the convergence of significant themes and phrases in Homer with those of neighboring cultures and the possible explanatory alternatives, including the influence of one set of cultural forms upon another, in search for answers to the questions of "when and how Greek poets learned these stories, and under what historical and archeological conditions."[5]

After reviewing the contribution of archeology to a greater understanding of the Near Eastern "Dark Age" period between 1200 BC and 700 BC, she comes to the important consideration that "Near Eastern influence could have flourished without writing and monumental art, during the survival of Bronze Age forms into Homeric poetry. For example, the Hittites had little archeologically visible contact with Mycenean Greece, yet their literary and ritual texts show close parallels to Homer."[6]

Another significant link between Homer and the Near East emerges in the field of religion. For Morris, the Iliadic interactions between Gods and humans have a strong Oriental flavor and the Homeric religion cannot be separated from the Near East; the pantheon and the division of the cosmos among the three brother gods is clearly Near Eastern in origin; the Iliadic sacrifices follow "purposes and procedures... long practiced in the

Bronze Age, including many described in the Bible"; Enkidu of the Gilgamesh epic dies before the major hero, as Patroclus does before Achilles; both the ghosts of Enkidu and of Patroclus appear around the end of the epics.

I opened this brief historical review by quoting the opening lines of Prof. Morris and I will close it with her closing statement:

> In the final analysis, it may be a greater challenge to isolate and appreciate what is Greek in Homeric poetry than to enumerate its foreign sources. Exploring the many treasures common to Homeric and Near Eastern epic, including the Hebrew Bible, enables modern readers to join archeologists and recover the lost unity of ancient Mediterranean literature and life.[7]

Prof. Morris is part of the western sociocultural basin. When she analyses in a broad sense the relationship between the Orient and the West, and examines the Oriental influences upon Greek archaic and classical literature, she focuses primarily on Homer as the prototypical representative of Greek epic poetry, although she also uses examples taken from the works of Hesiod. Her standing is consistent with the Western zeitgeist and the concept of essentialism that I have discussed earlier on. However, this socio-culturally dictated view does not diminish in any way her significant contribution to clarify the substantial Oriental flavor of Homer's affective stance. The Oriental influence would represent a similarly noteworthy factor if Homer were a born citizen of Mycenae, or Athens, rather than a possible orphan child—and carrying the emotional experience of being a young hostage—of Smyrna, or Chios. What would profoundly change, between these two alternatives, would be the magnitude and the affective significance of those influences in a Greek versus a non-Greek mind. And what would profoundly change the affective significance of the Near Eastern attractor would be whether the Trojan war was an event of conquest and heroic war deeds that happened in a distant land, or a tragic part of one's homeland history that carried devastating effects on its freedom and culture.

As Prof. Morris points out, "with notable exceptions, few classicists pursued Oriental connections in the last century."[8] It is likely that further discoveries among the vast trove of information about the Anatolian Bronze Age cultures, that was lost or destroyed during the Eastern Hellenistic infiltration, may further clarify the figure and role of Homer and his works.

Concurrently, the present psychological analysis will hopefully contribute to a more diversified assessment of future (and past!) material, linking the poet to his eastern origins and to the spirit of his time; and will illuminate the *Iliad* as a "song for Hector," an evocative dirge suffusing with poignant and tragic affect the descriptive façade of the "song for Achilles."

NOTES

1. Steinmetz Professor of Classical Archaeology and Material Culture Department of Classics, Cotsen Institute of Archaeology University of California at Los Angeles.
2. *A New Companion to Homer*, p. 599.
3. Ibid., p. 600
4. "The long-lived popularity of this story in the Near East, including its afterlife in the Bible, made it an heroic tradition as fundamental as Homer was to the Greek culture." (Ibid., p. 601).
5. Ibid., p. 606.
6. Ibid., p. 607.
7. Ibid., p. 623.
8. Ibid., p. 600.

Appendix A

I submit a limited synopsis concerning some of the material used for the psychodynamic reconstruction of Homer's mind and of the *Iliad*'s objectives.

It summarizes the most-quoted data on familial and environmental contributors to Homer's mental organization, and the retrieved developmental patterns of main Iliadic events and characters, indispensable for the formulation of a meaningful psychodynamic narrative; it mentions core dystonic aspects that call for a critical review of the theory that the *Iliad* was fundamentally a celebration of Achilles and Greek mighty; it provides some samples of Homeric comparisons used to clarify and reinforce a theme or to provide contrasting evidence; and it lists a few sample scenes in which Homer goes beyond the descriptive level and his emotional investment colors the narrative.

DEVELOPMENTAL PATTERNS

Homer

- His psychodynamic formulation is quintessential to the analytical understanding of his epic and its leading characters.
- Sources close to his time—who would still have shared a similar experience of living in the archaic Hellenistic world, with its sagas, philosophies, and religions—were the preferred ones in the search for data about his life.
- Later scholars modelled the image of the poet out of written versions of his epic, collected in their final forms at least six or seven centuries after his times, as in the Venetus A and B manuscripts.
- Apparently Homer was born within a few generations (2–4) from the collapse of the Trojan kingdom and of the free states of the western Anatolian seaboard (including his putative motherland).
- Fatherless product of illegitimate pregnancy (seduction? rape?).
- Mother: Cretheis (may have died soon after his birth), who lived in Old Smyrna and called him Melesigenes.
- As an infant or small child may have been offered/taken as hostage (homeros) to Smyrna or Chios, and the label/name stuck.
- Subject of Greek colonial power.
- Possibly subject to oneiric anxiety?

- Proficient in colonial (Homeric) Greek, rather than mainland Greek.

(As mentioned, the personal childhood experiences were analogically consistent with specific instances and references to children throughout the epic.)

The War

- The true cause was Zeus' concern with overpopulation (Schol. On Homer, Il. i. 5 #3, LCL #57, p. 497).
- The pretext was the competition for the golden apple, at the wedding of Peleus, among the goddesses Athene, Hera, and Aphrodite (LCL #57, p. 489–491).
- The precipitating event was the judgment of Paris that caused triumphant Aphrodite to beguile Helen into fleeing Sparta and following Paris, and the severe jealous wrath of Hera and Athene against Paris and Troy (Book XXIV, ll. 27 ff.).
- The consequence was the expedition borne out of the oath-bound obligation from all the pretenders to retrieve Helen for Menelaus.
- The first wrong expedition landed at Teuthras in Mysia ca. twenty years before the *Iliad* (Papyrus Oxy. LXIX 4708, verses by Archilochus).
- Ten years later a second expedition sailed from Aulis.
- Other nine years passed until the Iliadic summer.

Achilles

- Unwanted product of a forced and abhorred marriage.
- Divine mother tried at birth to change his humanity and make him immortal by alternatively burning him and anointing him with ambrosia.
- Parents practically divorced since his infancy.
- Grew up with his father. Powerful mother available on request.
- Was sent as a "πέμπε νήπιον," a five-year-old child, to the court of Agamemnon. possibly for rearing, training, and diplomacy. Developmentally, Achilles was at that time at the center of the phallic phase and in the midst of the Oedipus complex.
- Homer knew of this childhood connection; however, neither Achilles nor Agamemnon ever mention this past root to their relationship. Compare the sharing of past connections between Glaucos and Diomedes, or even Achilles and Lycaon!
- In the Cypria and related sagas, while still fifteen, he contained the defeat of the Achaean army at Teuthras by wounding the Mysian king Telephus.

- Later on, by healing Telephus, he provided the Achaeans with the correct location of Troy, a crucial key to the plans for a second expedition.
- Therefore, he likely felt entitled to a greater recognition and role than the ones he received by Agamemnon. His highly inflated sense of self—his wounded honor is more important than the fate of an army—may have even considered full leadership as the appropriate reward.
- In the *Iliad*, Achilles mentions, once, having a son (son's mother never mentioned), describes Briseis, once, as his beloved wife.
- Was too young to be a pretender to Helen's hand, therefore not bound by Tyndareus' oath.

Agamemnon

- At young age orphan of mother, who was thrown naked in the sea from a cliff by his father Atreus after he found that she had slept with his twin brother Thyestes.
- Was obliged to witness the killing of his mother, together with his younger brother Menelaus who cowered behind him.
- Obliged to participate to the dinner when Atreus, after he found out the adultery, served Thyestes with cooked bits of his children.
- Married Clytemnestra, Helen's sister, after killing her husband.
- A skillful politician, he was a major force behind the Mycenean golden age.

Patroclus

- As a child killed another child in a state of rage, during a game of dice.
- Was sent to Peleus to be purified and continued to live there, as an older brother figure to Achilles.
- Was given the role to tame Achilles' impulsive aggression.
- Had been a pretender to Helen's hand and therefore bound by the common oath.

Hector

- Oldest legitimate son of Priam and his chosen successor.
- Leader of the coalition among Trojans and allies.
- Predestined by Fate to be the ultimate protector of Troy.
- His death is necessary for the city to fall.
- Fully human, shows a gamma of emotions: mostly courage and bravery, but also moments of fear and cowardice.

- The best fighter among the Trojans, by the end of the *Iliad* has killed twenty-nine named Greeks.

The strife

- There are indications that the reciprocal animosity had been long-standing.
- It may have started during the time Achilles lived at Agamemnon's court. A fond, parent-child-like, relationship between them would have transpired at the beginning of the strike. Instead this earlier episode of their relationship is ignored except by Phoenix (*Iliad*, Book IX. ll. 438 ff.).
- Possible leadership conflict, already during first expedition.
- At Aulis Agamemnon had used Achilles as a betrothal bait to get Iphigenia from Mycenae. Achilles had become aware of it but was not able to stop the sacrifice, despite his assurance to Clytemnestra.
- Argument during journey to Troy about Achilles having been invited "late."

DYSTONIC ASPECTS

First question: about (appropriateness of) Achilles' anger:

- Lack of sustainable correlation between offense to his honor and required punishment.
- Briseis equal to sexual prize at best.
- Perceivable jealousy for leadership position.
- Repetitive and strong critical statements from all main Greek figures: Agamemnon, Odysseus, Aias, Phoenix, Diomedes, Patroclus.
- Cautioned by Hera and Athena.
- No support from the gods, eventually serious rejection, and disgust for Achilles' impious behavior.
- (The significant disparity between Greek and Trojan forces, the Myrmidons included, was not sufficient to conquer Troy during nine years of war.)

Second question: about Greek piety (devotional respect):

- Three present actual or potential instances of Greek impiety:
    - Agamemnon against Apollo.
    - Achilles against most gods about Hector.
    - (Achilles against Zeus about Priam).
- One at Aulis by Agamemnon boasting against Artemis.
- No instances of Trojan impiety.

- Repeated statements by Zeus about the great devotion of Priam and Hector.
- No corresponding praises of Greek devotion.

Samples of Comparisons

- Chryse to Priam (and Chryseis' — Hector's bodies).
- Achilles/Agamemnon to Achilles/Antilochus.
- Nestor to Trojan elders.
- Achilles' guilt for Achaeans to Hector's guilt for Trojans.
- Achilles/Briseis to Hector/Andromache.
- Hector/Andromache/Astyanax to Achilles/Neoptolemus/(wife).
- Zeus' strong response at Hector's grave injury to his unresponsiveness at Achilles' pleads for his own life.
- Troy's collective grief to Greek camp's collective grief.
- Patroclus' funeral to Hector's funeral.

Some situations with manifest affective cathexis:

- Chryses walking back along the seashore.
- The Achaean army being told to leave.
- Thersites.
- The encounter between Andromache and Hector.
- The seduction of Zeus.
- Achilles' acute grief.
- Briseis grief.
- The flooded Scamander field scene.
- Hector at the Scaean gate.
- The acute grief of Hecabe, Priam, and Andromache, and of the entire city.
- The visuals of the slaughtering at Patroclus' pyre.
- The chariot race.
- Priam's rescue mission, the tension in Achilles' hut, Priam back at the gate.
- The funeral rites with lamenting songs and the crying of a city.

Appendix B

Iliad *Books: A Synopsis*

BOOK I: THE PLAGUE AND THE STRIFE

King Agamemnon mistreats Chryse, a priest of Apollo. Apollo for nine days indiscriminately kills animals and men in the Greek camp. The seer Calchas, on request from Achilles, points to Agamemnon's act of impiety. The god demands that Chryses's daughter, captive Chryseis, be returned to her father. Agamemnon, who owns the woman, requests compensation. He and Achilles have a heated argument, Agamemnon takes Briseis, a captive of Achilles, as compensation. Achilles leaves the alliance and plans to return home. The elderly Nestor is introduced.

BOOK II: THE DREAM AND THE CATALOG OF THE SHIPS

Zeus sends to Agamemnon a false dream, promising that this day he will take Troy, after nine years of war. Homer then lists all the contingents of the 1,120 ships that form the fleet, naming each leader. He then briefly lists the army of the Trojans and their allies, and their respective leaders.

BOOK III: THE DUEL BETWEEN MENELAUS AND PARIS

Hector convinces Paris to duel with Menelaus in order to end the war. Both sides joyfully swear a truce and Priam sanctifies it. Paris is beaten but Aphrodite lifts him to Helen's bed before Menelaus could get to him and kill him.

BOOK IV: THE BREAKING OF THE TRUCE

Pressured by Hera's hatred at Troy Zeus arranges for the Trojan prince Pandarus to break the truce by wounding Menelaus with an arrow. The two sides begin to fight.

BOOK V: THE ARISTEIA OF DIOMEDES

Diomedes kills many Trojans and Pandaros, wounds Aeneas and Aphrodite who came to her son's rescue, and ultimately wounds Ares and puts him out of action.

BOOK VI: HECTOR AND ANDROMACHE

Hector rallies the Trojans. Diomedes and Lykian Glaukos share common ground and exchange unequal gifts. Hector enters Troy and bids farewell to his wife and child.

BOOK VII: THE BUILDING OF THE WALL

Hector and Ajax Telamon duel without a winner. The Greeks build a wall and a trench to protect their ships. The two sides collect and burn the dead.

BOOK VIII: THE BATTLE TO THE WALL

The Trojans push the Greeks to the wall before the coming of night stops them. They camp out and their watchfires light the plain like stars.

BOOK IX: THE EMBASSY TO ACHILLES

Agamemnon sends Odysseus, Ajax Telamon, and Phoenix to Achilles with incredible offerings, to persuade him to stop the strife. Achilles refuses and the embassy returns empty-handed.

BOOK X: THE FACTS OF DOLON

Later that night Odysseus and Diomedes infiltrate the Trojan lines, kill Dolon and scores of sleeping Thracians, including their king Rhesus.

BOOK XI: THE ARISTEIA OF AGAMEMNON

After fierce fighting Agamemnon, Diomedes, and Odysseus are wounded and retreat beyond the wall. Patroclus, sent by Achilles to inquire, speaks with Nestor.

BOOK XII: THE BATTLE BEYOND THE WALL

Hector leads the fighting on foot. The wall gate is broken with Sarpedon's help and Hector charges in.

BOOK XIII: THE BATTLE AT THE SHIPS

Many fall on both sides. The trojan seer Polydamas urges Hector to fall back and warns him against Achilles, but Hector ignores him.

BOOK XIV: HERA'S TRICK TO ZEUS

Hera seduces Zeus and lures him into sleep. Poseidon can then help the Greeks and the Trojans are driven back to the plain. Hector is gravely injured by a stone thrown at him by Great Ajax.

BOOK XV: THE TROJAN COUNTERATTACK

Zeus awakes, orders Poseidon to stop his support to the Greeks, sends Apollo to heal Hector and restore him to full strength, and to drive the Trojans who once again breach the wall and reach the ships. Hector and Ajax Telamon fight at the ship of Protesilaus.

BOOK XVI: THE DEEDS OF PATROCLUS

Patroclus, returns to the huts of Achilles and confronts his wrath and how much it is costing in Greek lives. Achilles begins to relent. At that time, Ajax falls back and Hector is able to put the ship on fire. Seeing this, Achilles rushes Patroclus to lead the Myrmidons and to don his armor as a disguise, but to return once the Trojans are drawn back beyond the wall. The Trojans are routed, the fire extinguished, but Patroclus keeps going toward Troy, kills Sarpedon on the way, attempts to storm the city, and is eventually killed by Hector.

BOOK XVII: THE DEEDS OF MENELAUS

Hector takes the armor of Patroclus but the body is protected by Menelaus, the two Ajaxes, and other Greek kings.

BOOK XVIII: THE MAKING OF THE DIVINE ARMOR

Achilles is informed that Patroclus has died. The Greeks are able to carry the corpse to the camp of the Myrmidons. Polydamas again counsels Hector to retreat behind the city walls, but Hector refuses. Thetis asks Hephaestus to forge a new armor for her son.

BOOK XIX: THE END OF THE STRIFE AGAINST THE GREEKS

Achilles and Agamemnon cease their strife. The gifts are presented to Achilles, including Briseis. The Greeks take their meal and rest while Achilles gets ready for battle.

BOOK XX: THE BATTLE IN THE PLAIN

Zeus lifts the ban on the gods' interference and the gods freely help both sides. Achilles slays many, confronts Aeneas and, briefly, Hector.

BOOK XXI: THE RIVERS AND GODS BATTLE

Achilles slays many in the river Scamander. The river god, angry, asks him to stop and then tries to drown him, joining forces with his brother the river Simois. Hera sends her son Hephaestus to stop the rivers with fire. The gods fight among themselves. The Trojans flee into the city while Apollo drives Achilles away by tricking him.

BOOK XXII: DEATH OF HECTOR

Hector, alone, refuses to find refuge inside the city. He flees from Achilles, running thrice around the city, until is tricked into a standing by Athena. Achilles kills him with his spear and drags his body, tied to his chariot, to the Greek camp.

BOOK XXIII: THE FUNERAL GAMES FOR PATROCLUS

The ghost of Patroclus urges Achilles to bury him. Achilles sacrifices animals and humans on the pyre, which initially fails to burn, and then holds a day of funeral games with the giving of prizes. Achilles continues to deface Hector's body.

BOOK XXIV: THE RANSOM AND BURIAL OF HECTOR

The dismayed Zeus commands that the body be returned and has Priam come to the Myrmidons' camp, guided by Hermes. Eventually Achilles relinquishes the body and Priam carries him back to Troy, where he receives a proper burial.

Bibliography

Aeschylus (vol. II). Translated by Smyth, Herbert W. Loeb Classic Library # 146. Cambridge, Mass., Harvard University Press, 2006.

Alexander, C. *The War That Killed Achilles: The True Story of Homer's* Iliad *and the Trojan War*. New York, Viking Penguin, 2009.

Apollodorus. *The Library*. Translated by J. G. Frazer, Loeb Classical Library # 121–122. Cambridge, Mass., Harvard University Press, 2001.

Apollonius Rhodius. *Argonautica*. Translated by W. H. Race, Loeb Classical Library # 1. Cambridge, Mass., Harvard University Press, 2008.

Beardslee W., Jacobson A., Hauser S., et al. *An Approach to Evaluating Adolescent Adaptive Processes: Scale Development and Reliability*. J. Am. Acad. Child Psychiatry 24: 637–642, 1985 (p. 177).

Beckman, G. *Hittite Diplomatic Texts*. Atlanta, Georgia, Scholar Press, 1999.

Beckman G, Bryce T., Cline E. *The Ahhiyawan Texts*. Atlanta, Georgia, Society of Biblical Literature, 2011.

Bedi, A. *Path to the Soul*, Weiser Books, 2000.

Bryce, T. *Life and Society in the Hittite World*. New York, Oxford University Press, 2004.

Bryce, T. *The Kingdom of the Hittites*. New York, Oxford University Press, 2005.

Cabaniss, D., et al., *Psychodynamic Formulation*. New York, Wiley-Blackwell, 2013.

Diodorus Siculus. The Library of History. Translated by C. H. Oldfather, Loeb Classical Library # 279. Cambridge, Mass., Harvard University Press, 2004.

Edelman, G. *Wider Than the Sky: The Phenomenal Gift of Consciousness*. New Haven, CT, Yale University Press, 2004.

Euripides. *Bacchae, Iphigenia at Aulis, Rhesus*. Translated by D. Kovacs, Loeb Classical Library # 495, Cambridge, Mass., Harvard University Press, 2002.

Gelernter, D. *The Muse in the Machine: Computerizing the Poetry of Human Thought*. New York, Free Press, 1994.

Harris W. H. *Ancient Literacy*. Cambridge, Mass., Harvard University Press, 1989.

Herodotus. *The Histories*. Translated by D. Grene. Chicago, The University of Chicago Press, 1987.

Hesiod. *The Homeric Hymns and Homerica*. Translated by Evelyn-White, Hugh G. Loeb Classic Library # 57. Cambridge, Mass., Harvard University Press, 1982.

Homer. *Iliade*. Traduzione di. Rosa Calzecchi Onesti. Einaudi, Torino, 1950.

Homer. *Iliad*. Translated by A.T. Murray. Loeb Classical Library 170–171. Cambridge, Mass., Harvard University Press, 1999.

Homer. The *Iliad*. Translated by A. Pope. Sydney, Australia, Wentworth Press, 2016.

Homer. The *Iliad* and The *Odyssey*. Translated by Samuel Butler. New York, Barnes and Noble Books, 1999.

Homer. The *Odyssey*. Translated by E.T. Murray, revised by G. E. Dimok Loeb Classical Library 104–105, Cambridge, Mass., Harvard University Press 1998.

Homeric Hymns, Homeric Apocrypha, Lives of Homer. Edited and translated by M. West. Loeb Classical Library # 496, Cambridge, Mass., Harvard University Press 2003.

Janko, R. *Homer, Hesiod and the Hymns*. Cambridge, Mass., Cambridge Classical Library, 1982.

Janko, R. *Intellectual Biography and Current Research*. Personal Homepage (public domain).

Jung, C. G. *The Red Book: Liber Novum*. Translated by M. Kybura, J. Peck, S. Shamdasani. Edited by Sonu Shamdasani. Philemon Series, New York, W.W. Norton, 2009.

Kaszniak, A. W. "Consciousness." In D. Levenson, J. J. Ponzetti, and P. F. Jorgenson (Eds.), *Encyclopedia of Human Emotions*. New York, Macmillan, 1999. From Sanguineti, *A Rosetta Stone of the Human Mind: Three Languages to Integrate Neurobiology and Psychology*, pp. 89 ff. New York, Springer Books, 2006.

King, K.C. *Achilles: Paradigms of the War Hero from Homer to the Middle Ages*. Berkeley, University of California Press, 1987.

Laband, J. *The Rise and Fall of the Zulu Nation*. London, Arms and Armour Press, 1997.

Lichtheim M. *Ancient Egyptian Literature, II: The New Kingdom*. Berkeley, University of California Press, 1976.

Morris, J., Powell, B. *A New Companion to Homer*. Netherlands, Koninklijke Brill NV Publisher, 2011.

Nagler, M.N. *Approaches to Teaching Homer's* Iliad *and* Odyssey. New York, Myrsiades, Kostas, Modern Language Association of America, 1987.

Sanguineti, V. "The Roles of Essentialism and Religion as Scaffolds to Terrorism." In *Before and after Violence*, S. Akhtar (ed.). Lanham, Md., Lexington Books, 2018.

Sanguineti, V. *The Rosetta Stone of the Human Mind; Three Languages to Integrate Neurobiology and Psychology*. New York, Springer, 2007.

Scott, A. *Neuroscience: A Mathematical Primer*. New York, Springer-Verlag, 2002.

Shay, J. *Achilles in Vietnam: Combat Trauma and the Undoing of Character*. New York, Scribner Book Co., 1994.

Thucydides. *The Peloponnesian War*. Translated by Thomas Hobbes. Chicago, University of Chicago Press, 1989.

Wood, R. *An Essay on the Original Genius and Writings of Homer*. London, H. Hughes for T. Payne & P. Elmsly, 1775.

Index

Achilles, 23, 27n20, 29–46, 63, 82n45; Briseis and, 46, 52n84; as commander, 33, 49n23; depiction of, 45; developmental patterns, 85, 112–113; dystonic aspects of, 114; friends of, 41–42, 51n61; glorification of, 44–45, 103, 106n18, 106n19, 106n20; Hector, Priam and, 76–79; on Helen, 97, 105n2; as hero, 37; honor, 42, 43, 52n65, 67; libidinal energy, 65, 80n14; obstinacy of, 41–43; relationship with Patroclus, 64–65, 66–67, 69, 80n7, 80n9; testimony to, 75, 83n67; wrath, 30–32, 33, 40, 73, 76, 85, 114; young, 43, 105n12
action, impulse and, 75
acts, of impiety, 57, 60n12, 90, 114
actualization, self, 2
Aegean Sea, 18
Aegisthus, 91
Aeneas, 70
Aeschylus, 50n46, 94n19
affective cathexis, dystonic aspects of, 115
"affect linking," 24, 27n22, 35
Agamemnon, 29–31, 45, 52n80, 86, 92; depiction of, 37, 40, 51n52; developmental patterns, 113; impiety of, 37, 38–39, 48n4, 50n41, 50n48; as paternal substitute, 43; strife and, 40
aggression, 34, 86
Aias Telamon, 44, 86
Alexander, Caroline, 19, 20, 21, 33
Alexander the Great (king), 1
allied forces, 59, 60n6, 60n7, 60n8, 60n9, 60n10
analysis: of armies, 55–60; descriptive, 29–32, 100–102; dynamic, 33–36, 55–60; limited, 75
Anatolia, Turkey, 8
Andromache, 77, 81n33, 99
animal similes, 58–59, 61n14
animus archetypes, 65, 80n17
Antilochus, 82n35, 106n21
Aphrodite (deity), 87
Apollo (deity), 30, 90, 100, 105n11
Appiah, Kwame Anthony, 26n19
archeology, 108
archetypes, 5, 6, 39, 79; animus, 65, 80n17; male, 35
Argonautica (Rhodius), 33–34
Aristarchus, 83n75
aristeia, Homer and Achilles, 70–76
armies: Book II analysis of, 55–60; descriptions, 55–56, 60n6, 60n7, 60n9, 60n10
armor, 67–68, 80n1
arousal dimensions, 24, 27n25, 59
art, literary, structures of, 100
Artemis (deity), 37–38
aspects, deities, 91, 92, 93, 95n27, 95n28. *See also* dystonic aspects
assembly, 33
assessment: diversified, 109; of *Iliad*, 1; psychological, of Book XXIV, 102–105
Assuwan Confederacy, 15n24
Athene (deity), 74, 80n6, 83n61, 83n62, 89–90, 94n16
attitudes, conflicting, 57–58
attractors, 24, 27n21, 81n25, 93
audiences, 18, 25n2
Aulis, 37, 50n47

basins, sociocultural, 5, 6, 90, 93, 109
battle, descriptions, 44, 70–71
Bedi, Ashok, MD, 105
Bergen, Norman, 81n30

125

body, 79; counts, 75–76, 83n68; of Hector, 76, 77, 78, 83n71, 84n78; symbolism of, 79
Book I (*Iliad*), 29–32; main characters in, 37–41, 50n39; opening demands, 33–36, 85, 87; strife in, 37–41, 51n51; synopsis, 117
Book II (*Iliad*): opposing armies analysis, 55–60; synopsis, 117
Book III (*Iliad*), 117
Book IV (*Iliad*), 117
Book IX (*Iliad*): strife and wrath, 41–45; synopsis, 118
Book V (*Iliad*), 118
Book VI (*Iliad*), 118
Book VII (*Iliad*), 118
Book VIII (*Iliad*), 118
Book X (*Iliad*), 118
Book XI (*Iliad*), 118
Book XII (*Iliad*), 119
Book XIII (*Iliad*), 119
Book XIV (*Iliad*), 119
Book XIX (*Iliad*), 63–64; Patroclus role in, 64–68; synopsis, 120
Book XV (*Iliad*), 119
Book XVI (*Iliad*), 119
Book XVII (*Iliad*), 119
Book XVIII (*Iliad*), 120
Book XX (*Iliad*), 70, 120
Book XXI (*Iliad*), 120
Book XXII (*Iliad*), 73, 120
Book XXIII (*Iliad*), 120
Book XXIV (*Iliad*): descriptive analysis, 100–102; psychological assessment, 102–105; synopsis, 121
Briseis, 63, 65; Achilles and, 46, 52n84; as prize, 47, 50n37
burning ships, 67, 81n23
Butler, S., 92

Cabaniss, D., MD, 2–3, 3, 93n1
Calchas, 30, 37
cannibalism, 74, 75, 83n65, 83n66
cathexis, affective, dystonic aspects of, 115
causality, of wrath, 45–48
characters: in Book I, 37–41, 50n39; qualities of, 86; *See also specific characters*

chariots, 47, 53n89, 70
chief leadership, 45–46
childhood, of Homer, 7–8, 9
child psyche, 23–24
children, Trojan, 97, 105n3
choice, of words, 46–47, 52n85
cities, destruction of, 104, 106n22
civilizations, x, 104
classicists, 109
closing lines, 48n1, 105
Clytemnestra, 38, 50n44
cognitive disconnectedness, 35
cognitive tapestry, 24, 27n24
collective grief, 23, 76–77, 83n73, 102, 103
collective memories, 6–7, 13n5
colonization, 8, 12
combined self, 66
commander, Achilles as, 33, 49n23
companion, Patroclus as, 65
comparisons, dystonic aspect, 115
compensation, 39, 51n49
complex language, 58
conclusions, 45–48; grief in, 100
conflicts, 37–38, 50n45; attitudinal, 57–58; intrapersonal, 69–70
confrontational relationships, 41
confrontations, 37
contrasts, 99
counts, body, 75–76, 83n68
creativity, 58
criticism, 66
culture: differences of, x; eulogy to, 104, 105; religious, 88; Western, ix
current, of emotions, 103
Cypria (poem), 14n11, 37, 50n40

daimons, 98, 99
damaged self, 69
Damasio, Antonio, 6, 13n3
data, 3–4, 13, 58, 102, 111
death penalty, 82n34
deception, 42
"deep bosomed," women, 36, 50n36
defacement, of Hector, 100, 105n11
Deidameia, 105n12
deities, 35–36, 49n30, 49n33, 49n34, 72, 81n28; interventions, 87–88, 94n5; similarities between, 88, 91, 92; two-

faced aspects, 91, 92, 93, 95n27, 95n28; *See also specific deities*
demands, opening, 33–36
depiction: of Achilles, 45; of Agamemnon, 37, 40, 51n52
depths, psychological, 3, 81n25, 100–101
descriptions: armies, 55–56, 60n6, 60n7, 60n9, 60n10; battle, 44, 70–71
descriptive analyses, 29–32, 100–102
destruction, of cities, 104, 106n22
"destructive dream," 41, 51n55, 55
developmental patterns, 111–114; Achilles, 112–113; Agamemnon, 113; Hector, 113–114; Homer, 111–112; Patroclus, 113; strife, 114; Trojan War, 112
dialects, Greek, 14n14
differences, cultural, x
dimensions: arousal, 24, 27n25, 59; divine, 34, 35, 49n34, 72, 87–93, 92–93; of grief, 101–102, 103–104; valence, 23, 27n25, 46, 59
Diodorus, 15n29
disconnectedness, cognitive, 35
disparity, between forces, 56, 57
dissonance, 20
diversified assessment, 109
divine dimension, 34, 35, 49n34, 72, 87–93, 92–93
duels, 74, 83n63
dynamic analyses, 33–36, 55–60
dynamic processes, 3
dystonic aspects: of Achilles, 114; of affective cathexis, 115; comparisons, 115; of piety, 114–115

Edelman, G., 27n23
ego/superego structure, 67, 81n20, 81n21, 81n22
elders, Trojan, 97, 105n1
elements, 72
emotions, current of, 103
empathy, 24, 45, 65, 77
enchantment, 22, 23
envy, 41
Epic Cycle, 2, 10, 21–22, 92; as fragmentary, 58; Neoanalysts on, 15n22

Epic of Gilgamesh (poem), 41, 51n58, 108, 109, 110n4
Eratosthenes, 10, 13n2
essentialism, 23, 26n19, 109
ethical landscape, of Troy, 98
etymology, 33, 49n22
eulogy, to culture, 104, 105
events, pivotal, 17–18
evolution, psychodynamic, 15n26
expansionism, 6, 8, 102–103
expressions, of grief, 104

fate, 17, 74, 83n61, 87
fathers, 78–79
feelings, 2, 3, 25
the feminine, 33, 49n25, 65–66
figures, idealized, 19, 25n7
flood, great, traditions, 41, 108
Foley, John, 11
forces: allied, 59–60; disparity between, 56, 57; lists of, 55–56, 60n7, 60n9, 60n10
formulaic language, 24, 27n26
formulations, psychodynamic, 2–3
fragments, Epic Cycle in, 58
Freud, Sigmund, 4, 6, 38, 65, 75, 85
friends, of Achilles, 41–42, 51n61
funerals: Hector, 102; Patroclus, 103

Gelernter, D., 27n22
generations, 6–7
gestalt, 20, 66
Gilgamesh, Epic of (poem), 41, 51n58, 108, 109, 110n4
glimpses, into Troy, 97–100
glorification, of Achilles, 44–45, 103, 106n18, 106n19, 106n20
great flood traditions, 41, 108
Greek: dialects, 14n14; heroes, 86; written, 9, 14n15
grief, 80n3, 83n60, 83n74; as brief, 78, 84n76; collective, 23, 76–77, 83n73, 102, 103; as conclusion, 100; dimensions of, 101–102, 103–104; expressions of, 104
guilt, 69, 73–74

Haslam, M., 14n19
Hattusa (city), 22

Hecabe, 75, 83n65, 94n16, 104
Hector, 44, 57, 60n13, 68, 73; Achilles, Priam and, 76–79; Andromache and, 99; body of, 76, 77, 78, 83n71, 84n78; defacement of, 100, 105n11; developmental patterns, 113–114; funeral of, 102; on Paris, 98; symbolism of, 101
Helen, 68, 81n31, 105n2; song of, 98–99; Trojan elders on, 97, 105n1
Hephaestus (deity), 63, 72, 80n3, 82n54, 82n55
Hera (deity), 33, 49n24, 94n9, 94n18; Homer on, 89, 91; Zeus and, 89, 94n12, 94n14
hero: Achilles as, 37; Greek, 86
hero-animus, 65
Herodotus, 12
Hesiod, The Homeric Hymns and Homerica, 4n1
historians, 12
history, 17–18, 58, 106n23, 107–108
Hittite Diplomatic Texts, 14n12
home, returning, 55, 60n3, 60n5
Homer, ix–x, 1, 1–2, 4n1; Achilles aristeia and, 70–76; on causality of wrath, 45–48; childhood of, 7–8, 9; developmental patterns, 111–112; divine dimension and, 87–93, 92–93; on Hera, 89, 91; mental organization of, 111; on Zeus, 89; *See also specific topics*
Homer and the Near East (Morris), 107–108, 108–109
honor, 40; Achilles, 42, 43, 52n65, 67; injured, 47, 48

idealized figures, 19, 25n7
Iliad (Homer), ix, 1, 13n6; assessment of, 1; closing lines, 48n1, 105; interpretations of, x; limits of, 59; manuscripts of, 9–10, 14n18; opening lines, 29; tenderness of, 99; as tragedy, 2, 103; *See also specific books; specific topics*
illegitimate pregnancy, 7, 14n8
Illuminism, 107
immigrants, 9

impiety, 36, 41, 78, 93; acts of, 57, 60n12, 90, 114; of Agamemnon, 37–38, 39, 48n4, 50n41, 50n48
impulse, action and, 75
influences, Oriental, 107–109
injured honor, 47, 48
inspiration, 17, 23
insults, 31, 49n15
interpretations: of *Iliad*, x; poetic, 26n11
interventions, deities, 87–88, 94n5
intrapersonal conflicts, 69–70
Iris (deity), 55

Janko, R., 9, 20
Jung, Carl, x, 4, 5–6

Kaszniak, A., 27n25
King, K. C., 106n20
kingdoms, 8, 26n13
kings, 40, 51n53

language: complex, 58; formulaic, 24, 27n26
leadership, 45–46, 70
letter, Tawagalawa, 14n13
Liber Primus (Jung), 5
libidinal energy, Achilles, 65, 80n14
librarians, 10
limited analysis, 75
limits, of *Iliad*, 59
Linear B (written Greek), 9, 14n15
lines: closing, 48n1, 105; opening, 29
lions, 58–59, 61n14
lists, 42, 51n64, 55–56, 60n6, 60n7, 60n9, 60n10
literacy, 15n23
literary art, structures of, 100
The Lives of Homer (collective texts), 7–8
living forces, 36
loss, 47
Lycaon, 71
Lyrnessus (fortress), 57

magic, 2, 4n3
main characters, in Book I, 37–41, 50n39
male archetype, 35
mantle, of Priam, 101, 106n14
manuscripts, *Iliad*, 9–10, 14n18

masculine, feminine and, 65–66
Medjedovic, Avdo, 11
Melos, 12
Memnon (king), 60
memories, 6–7, 13n5, 100
Menelaus, 88
menis (wrath), 33
mental organization, of Homer, 111
methodologies, multidimensional, 3
milieu, sociocultural, 18, 19, 25
models, psychological, 4
Morris, S., 13, 107–108, 108–109
motherland, 7
motives, 25n3
multidimensional methodologies, 3
Murray, A. T., 19
mutiny, 55, 57, 60n4
mythology, 6, 107–108

Near Eastern history and mythology, 107–108
Neoanalysts, 15n22
Nestor, 31, 32, 41, 49n21, 51n60, 64
"nostalgy," ix, x

obstinacy, of Achilles, 41–43
Odysseus, 42, 92
Odyssey (Homer), ix, 1–2
oedipal triumph, 48
Oedipus Complex, 85
offerings, 89, 94n7
Old Smyrna, 21, 26n14
opening demands, Book I, 33–36
opening lines, 29
opposing armies analysis, Book II, 55–60
Oral Formulaic Theory, 11
oral poems, 1
oral traditions, 10–12, 13, 21
organization, mental, of Homer, 111
Oriental influences, 107–109
original sources, 4
orphanhood, 77

Paris, 87–88, 94n3, 94n6, 98
parricide, 37, 85
Parry, Milman, 11
passion, 20
paternal substitute, Agamemnon as, 43

Patroclus, 64, 68, 80n8, 81n32; Book XIX role of, 64–68, 81n25; developmental patterns, 113; as empathic companion, 65; funeral, 103; relationship with Achilles, 64–65, 66–67, 69, 80n7, 80n9
patterns, developmental. *See* developmental patterns
Pelides. *See* Achilles
penalty, death, 82n34
phase-space attractors, 24, 27n21, 93
Phoenix, 43, 44, 51n62
piety, dystonic aspects of, 114–115
pivotal events, 17–18
poems, ix; Cypria, 14n11, 37, 50n40; Epic of Gilgamesh, 41, 51n58, 108, 109, 110n4; Trojan Poem, 25n1
poetic interpretations, 26n11
polytheistic systems, 35–36, 49n30, 49n33, 49n34
Pope, A., 14n20
post-traumatic stress disorder (PTSD), 18
pregnancy, illegitimate, 7, 14n8
Priam, 68, 73, 84n77, 101; Hector, Achilles and, 76–79; mantle of, 101, 106n14
priestesses, 90
prize, 47–48, 53n86, 53n88, 106n21; Briseis as, 47, 50n37; women as, 30, 36, 40, 50n36
processes, dynamic, 3
projection, 56–57, 69
projective regression, 68, 69, 82n40
prophet, 30
psyches: child, 23–24; Western collective, 19
psychic systems, 18, 25n4
psychodynamic evolution, 15n26
psychodynamic formulations, 2–3
psychological assessment, of Book XXIV, 102–105
psychological depths, 3, 81n25, 100–101
psychological models, 4
PTSD. *See* post-traumatic stress disorder

qualities, of characters, 86

Raaflaub, K., 6
Race in the Modern World (Appiah), 26n19
races, chariots, 47, 53n89
Ramesses II (pharaoh), 93n2
realities, subjective, 56–57
regression, projective, 68, 69, 82n40
relationships: confrontational, 41; Patroclus and Achilles, 64–65, 66–67, 69, 80n7, 80n9; "three-persons relationship," 85, 93n1
religion, 108–109
religious cultures, 88
renewal, Trojan, 105, 106n23
repression, 65
resentment, 46
returning home, 55, 60n3, 60n5
revenge, 69, 71, 74, 82n34, 82n48
revisionism, 4, 10, 14n20
rhapsodes, 10, 22
Rhea (deity), 87, 94n4
Rhodius, Apollonius, 33–34
ruse, 55, 60n1

sacrifices, 35, 49n29, 63, 71
sagas, 92
Samothrace, 10
Sanguineti, V.R., MD, 26n19, 27n21
sarcasm, 66
Scott, A., 27n21
self: actualization, 2; combined, 66; damaged, 69
self-condemnation, 70
semasiography, 15n21
senseless war, 55
Shay, J., 18, 20, 26n11, 39–40
ships, 55, 56, 67, 81n23
similarities, between deities, 88, 91, 92
similes, 58–59, 61n14, 80n18, 82n57
Sirius (star), 73, 82n57
sociocultural basins, 5, 6, 90, 93, 109
sociocultural milieu, 18, 19, 25
soldiers, Vietnam, 69, 80n13, 82n36, 82n39
song, of Helen and Paris, 98–99
sources, original, 4
spears, 74, 83n62
"spirit of the time," 5, 14n20, 19, 20, 35, 57–58
splitting, 82n40
Stasinus of Cyprus, 37, 50n40
strife, 34, 36, 63, 67; Agamemnon and, 40; Book I, 37–41, 51n51; Book IX, 41–45; developmental patterns, 114; Shay on, 39–40; variables of, 45, 46
structures, 27n24; ego/superego, 67, 81n20, 81n21, 81n22; of literary art, 100
studies, 18
subjective realities, 56–57
substitute, paternal, Agamemnon as, 43
symbolism: of bodies, 79; of Hector, 101
symmetry, 78, 79
systems: polytheistic, 35–36, 49n30, 49n33, 49n34; psychic, 18, 25n4

tapestry, cognitive, 24, 27n24
Tarkasnawa of Mira (king), 21
Tawagalawa letter, 14n13
tears, 66, 80n18
Telephus, 46, 52n81
tenderness, of *Iliad*, 99
terrorism, x
testimony, to Achilles, 75, 83n67
themes, 32, 33, 34–35, 79–80, 93
thoughts, 3
"three-persons relationship," 85, 93n1
topography, 22, 23, 26n15, 26n16
traditions: great flood, 41, 108; oral, 10–12, 13, 21
tragedy, *Iliad* as, 2, 103
transferred wrath, 68–70
translations, 26n11
trauma, 8
triumph, oedipal, 48
Trojan children, 97, 105n3
Trojan elders, 97, 105n1
Trojan Poem, 25n1
Trojan renewal, 105, 106n23
Trojan War, 8, 12, 13, 17, 21–22, 112
Troy, 22, 23; ethical landscape of, 98; glimpses into, 97–100; Zeus and, 98
Turner, Frank, 18
two-faced aspects, deities, 91, 92, 93, 95n27, 95n28

valence dimensions, 23, 27n25, 46, 59
variables, of strife, 45, 46
Venetus A and B (*Iliad* manuscripts), 9–10, 14n18
Vietnam soldiers, 69, 80n13, 82n36, 82n39

war, 1; senseless, 55; Trojan War, 8, 12, 13, 17, 21–22, 112
Western Canon, 5, 13n1
Western collective psyche, 19
Western culture, ix
wisdom, of Nestor, 41
women: "deep bosomed," 36, 50n36; as prizes, 30, 36, 40, 50n36
words, 24, 46–47, 52n85

wrath, 63, 91; Achilles, 30–32, 33, 40, 73, 76, 85, 114; Book IX, 41–45; causality of, 45–48; transferred, 68–70
wrath (*menis*), 33
writers, ix
written Greek, 9

Xanthus (river), 71, 72
Xerxes (king), 56

young Achilles, 43, 105n12

Zenodotus, 1, 10
Zeus (deity), 39, 55, 60n1, 74, 83n58, 83n60, 83n61; Hera and, 89, 94n12, 94n14; Homer on, 89; Troy and, 98

About the Author

Vincenzo Sanguineti was born in Eritrea and lived there until completion of medical school at the "Universita' Degli Studi" in Milan, Italy, where he also held a position as Instructor at the Department of Physiology. In Eritrea he carried out anthropological studies for the Institute of Psychology of Milan University. He then spent five years in Nigeria, where he conducted published field research in tropical medicine, participated to the medical services for the building of a hydroelectric dam on the Niger River, and directed a missionary hospital. Consequently, he profited from the prolonged exposure to uncontaminated natural habitats and to the degrees of difference and similarity among different species, and different human cultures. He moved to the United States in 1970, completed his training in psychiatry at Yale and was a member of its faculty until 1989, when he relocated to Philadelphia and joined Jefferson Medical College. He had always experienced a deep interest and fascination for the interaction between the unique subjectivity of the self and the interactive processes stemming from the profound complexity of the individual and collective variables participating to the phase-space of the mind. These variables represent a combination of the specific sociocultural characteristics and rules of each epoch (what Jung defined as the spirit of the time) and of the eternal unchanging domain of the archetypes, those cognitive and affective configurations that represent the world of the organizing templates and are untouched by the passage of time. Jung called this domain the spirit of the depth. The Jungian concepts added to the author's prolonged experience of different cultures and enriched his deep interest in history, particularly at sociocultural intersections, as was the case with the Trojan saga.

Such interests evolved into more programmatic research and generated various studies and presentations at national and international conventions, as well as forming the basis of his books: *Landscapes in My Mind*, *The Rosetta Stone of the Human Mind*, and the present analysis of Homer, as well as chapters in several scholarly works; and of his fictional historical biography of Sarpedon, the mythical king of Lykia and great hero at Troy.

Presently, Dr. Sanguineti is in private practice and an associate professor of psychiatry at Jefferson Medical College.

www.ingramcontent.com/pod-product-compliance
Lightning Source LLC
Chambersburg PA
CBHW070832300426
44111CB00014B/2532